The Innovative School Librarian

SECOND EDITION

Every purchase of a Facet book helps to fund
CILIP's advocacy, awareness and accreditation programmes
for information professionals.

The Innovative School Librarian

SECOND EDITION

Sharon Markless, editor
Elizabeth Bentley, Sarah Pavey,
Sue Shaper, Sally Todd, Carol Webb

facet
publishing

Published by Facet Publishing,
7 Ridgmount Street, London WC1E 7AE
www.facetpublishing.co.uk

Facet Publishing is wholly owned by CILIP: the Chartered Institute
of Library and Information Professionals.

British Library Cataloguing in Publication Data
A catalogue record for this book is available from the British Library.

ISBN 978-1-78330-055-6 (paperback)
ISBN 978-1-78330-106-5 (hardback)
e-ISBN 978-1-78330-147-8

First published 2009
This second edition 2016

Text printed on FSC accredited material.

Typeset from editors' files by Flagholme Publishing Services in 11/16pt
Aldine 401 and URW Grotesk.
Printed and made in Great Britain by CPI Group (UK) Ltd, Croydon,
CR0 4YY.

Contents

Preface

Katya received a visit by fellow librarians to see the new school library. She prepared for the visit by displaying information on all her most recent activities to demonstrate how the library contributed to assessment for learning, reader development, teaching of 16–18 year olds and staff training. Katya observed that her visitors wanted to look at her stock and her general displays and to discuss how she managed overdue books. Several times she drew their attention to the information that showcased her wider activities but the majority of her visitors remained focused on the room's resources and its management rather than moving to a discussion of teaching and learning.

Although the context of school librarianship has changed dramatically over the past seven years, we believe that the fundamental concerns introduced in this vignette, which opened the first edition of this book in 2009, remain the same. School librarians are still faced with difficult decisions about their roles, priorities and activities: the shape of their contribution to teaching and learning within their schools. Therefore in this second edition we still aim to prompt school librarians to stand back from their day-to-day activity and critically re-examine their values, philosophy and what defines their professional practice. We have maintained our focus on ways of thinking about the job of school librarian rather than on its operational responsibilities. However we do not underplay the changes that have occurred since 2009 and recognize the many different ways in which context affects what we do and what we are able to achieve. In response we discuss the challenges and opportunities accorded by such changes as burgeoning technologies and resource cuts, and offer new vignettes describing current situations.

We recognize that there are big differences between schools: different curricula, different patterns of governance and management; and different levels and types of resources, before we even get to the students and teachers. This inevitably leads to big differences between school libraries. However, through working internationally with colleagues from the USA, Australia, Sweden, Denmark, Lithuania and Portugal, we know that school librarians share many common concerns as well as a common vision of what we are trying to achieve. We therefore believe that this book has international relevance because although the authors are school librarians working in the UK and use UK examples, the book addresses principles and issues that all school librarians need to confront during their career, whatever their context.

We invite you to take what you want from this book and adapt the ideas to your own context. We are not trying to provide solutions to your everyday problems. We are challenging you as a school librarian to think more widely, to be strategic and to move outside your comfort zone into the heart of teaching and learning in your school. But we are also challenging you to do this in a way that connects deeply to your underpinning beliefs about the role of the school library and school librarian. To this end, the book raises issues to consider, questions to pose, and approaches to analysing your role. We hope that this will enable you to examine your practice critically and find the innovative responses that will work for you.

We have tried to illuminate the ideas in this book through vignettes that present some real experiences of school librarians. We hope that the vignettes will resonate with you and enable you to look afresh at elements of your own practice. The vignettes may indicate a way forward or the unexpected consequences of a course of action. However, they are not meant to be blueprints for action nor do we use them to suggest that everyone will find themselves in the situations outlined.

This book was written collaboratively by five school librarians and a lecturer in higher education. The school librarians work in very different environments (schools with different types of students, different rationales for the school library, different roles for the school library, different priorities and different governance). This collaboration involved us in a sustained quest for clarity and understanding. The process of collaboration forced us to share our assumptions, examine our prejudices and justify our interpretations. Effective collaboration is not about gaining consensus, but about crafting something more than can be achieved individually. Our different realities have been brought to bear on each chapter. The challenge has been to find significant things to say that all of us are happy to subscribe to.

How to read this book

We hope that you will read the chapters in this book in the order that they are presented. This is because we believe that coming to think and act differently is a cumulative experience; we have therefore constructed this book as a narrative designed to lead the reader through a succession of issues, culminating in the chapter on innovation, which we see as the key to renewing and refreshing our professional identities.

Sharon Markless (editor), Elizabeth Bentley, Sarah Pavey, Sue Shaper, Sally Todd, Carol Webb

Acknowledgements

Several of the vignettes arose from discussions on the School Librarians' Network, an online discussion forum. Many thanks to everyone who contributed.

We would like to thank David Streatfield for his helpful contributions when reading the draft version of this book.

PART 1

WHO IS THE LIBRARIAN?

CHAPTER 1

Professionalism and the school librarian

Why should professionalism be important to us? This has always been a hotly debated topic, across all sectors of librarianship because of its links to status, conduct and quality of service. In recent years we have been travelling through a global economic downturn, which combined with changes in UK government policy has resulted in a rapidly changing educational environment. In order to negotiate our identity within this context we need to make difficult choices, amid a plethora of changing expectations. This chapter will examine professionalism in the belief that it remains fundamental to our work identities.

How do we develop these identities and how do they link to our practice of librarianship?

When writing eight years ago, it was within the context of campaigning in the UK for statutory recognition of school libraries. Now we write at a time when library services in many sectors are being reduced or closed and so discussion of this issue of professionalism is ever more important. Indeed, many schools around the world are not fortunate enough to have a library and those that exist may not have statutory status or be run by someone with a librarianship qualification which results in provision of uneven quality. They may be run by teachers, teaching assistants, clerical assistants or volunteers who bring to the role a variety of qualifications and experience. The professional organization for librarians in the UK – the Chartered Institute of Library and Information Professionals (CILIP) – has moved towards promoting and implementing a framework of qualifications and accreditation, which covers the whole spectrum of those working in our field. There are different stages available on the same road of continuing professional development: Certification, Chartership and Fellowship (CILIP 2014a). Following this pathway or maintaining our footfall on it through the re-validation process, regardless of our starting point, demonstrates our commitment to professionalism.

If we cannot think about professionalism in terms of qualifications, experience or the promise of statutory status, where does that leave our ideas of professionalism? Traditionally we may view the general characteristics of a professional as altruistic, principled and ethical. Membership of a professional organization usually entails the upholding of a charter that sets out a code of conduct and standards to be maintained. Professional people may build up a sense of autonomy derived from their beliefs, ideals and standards, which lead them where necessary to stand in opposition to authority or even state control. The reality of the modern world is complex and notions of professionalism are more open to varied interpretation than they were in the past.

In this discussion there is another element that must be considered: identity. This has several layers, adding complications and requiring some reflection.

What influences the school librarian's professional identity?

Professionalism is not about status but about establishing worth, and that can only be conferred by those using the library service. Our professional identity is not only a personal construct but affected by and in a sense co-created by those around us. This is explored in a number of ways in Chapter 2. Insight can be gained from examining how others see us and our practice. One of the ways this can be done is by looking at the ways in which they construct our role. Job descriptions are a concrete expression of espoused values and can be used as a trigger for dialogue about our roles. To study job descriptions in greater depth we would recommend looking at *CILIP Guidelines for Secondary School Libraries* (Shaper, 2014).

The work environment

The work environment, with its intricate rituals and pressures, is a microcosm of wider society. The social and political realities of our work relationships can present enjoyment, satisfaction, bewilderment, alienation and heartache. The nature of the organization affects our professional identity. In some schools, the librarian is seen as the keeper of books, in others, as someone working at the heart of the learning process. One of the strongest influences will be the lead set by the head teacher. His or her vision of education and how far it permeates the senior leadership team is fundamental to the organization and the librarian's place within it.

Lia Kanton's head teacher gave an assembly for World Book Day about his reading habits and began by saying that he always asks Ms Kanton in the library to choose some books for his teenage son because she knows all the latest ones and never fails to find something that really suits him.

This head teacher invested Lia with authority in the minds of his audience. Within a school, everyone will have different views of the librarian, influenced by their previous experiences and the attitudes of those around them.

Our confidence and effectiveness in responding to the range of demands made, develops our professional identity in the eyes of others, so too do our image and appearance. This does not refer to the power-dressing concept of the 1980s, but to group theory. If we want to be part of a group, then we need to adopt their characteristics. If the leaders in our organization dress smartly, then we should do the same to be identified with their values.

Our professional identity

Our underlying purpose and values create the professional identity we wish to perpetuate. Where these are unclear to others the visibility of our role within the school is adversely affected. This is where a deeper consideration of group theory can take our understanding to the next level. Forsyth (2006) describes the stages of Tuckman's theory of group development as forming, storming, norming, performing and adjourning. At this point we will focus on stage 2: 'storming', which refers to engagement and intellectual conflict with each other; it is where appreciation of other viewpoints is gained and jointly understood meanings are achieved. Ideally this process helps provide individuals with insight into ways forward, establishing norms in order to achieve the group goals (norming); conversely it can also highlight reasons why a group is unable to work well together. One cannot reach successful 'performance' without developing those relationships.

The importance of this concept is underlined by the findings of research into teachers' understanding of information literacy (Williams and Wavell, 2006b). This found that although teachers understood information literacy to be a useful consideration they found the linear models used by librarians to be too prescriptive and simplistic. These models were more about the practice of information literacy in a library context than that used in the classroom. In learning from this research, librarians continue to engage with teachers to find ways within their subject contexts to develop student skills. Tuckman (quoted in Forsyth, 2006) emphasizes that some of his stages are cyclical, so 'storming' may be a continual process for teachers and librarians to explore and negotiate meanings. Our professional role cannot be understood by teachers unless we engage intellectually with them.

How we are received and treated reinforces our professional identity and in this context the concept of cognitive authority is particularly relevant to librarians working in the education sector. Cognitive authority (Wilson, 1983) is concerned with how people construct knowledge from their experience and the ideas of other people. The term cognitive authority is applied to a person or source of information that is seen as credible and therefore is allowed to have influence over one's thinking. If a colleague who is seen as authoritative by others introduces us as an expert, then they extend their authority to us. This was illustrated in the vignette about Lia whose head teacher referred to her as a source of expertise for reading recommendations. This conferring of authority establishes our professional identity in the eyes of students and colleagues. Subsequently, as established staff members we can similarly confer cognitive authority on others.

We bring different qualities to the role and identity of school librarian from our previous career experiences. Indeed some of us believe that the solo librarianship experience, common in schools, can be a gruelling one for a young professional. Well developed professional experience may be an advantage in such situations. Reasons for job choice affect our engagement and motivation in the post and this is reflected in the development of our professional identity. Whatever our background, the difficulties of this challenging role should not be underestimated. Further complications may arise when we enter an organization where the predominant view of the librarian's role is at odds with our personal vision. This will be explored further in Chapter 3.

One way forward is to consider the issues identified in different discourses of professionalism. These give us indicators about what professional practice looks like and what we are doing when we act professionally. There are many different models and each has strengths and weaknesses. They help us to examine ourselves as professionals in our schools and give us ways of moving on. Their influences help determine our priorities for how time and money should be spent in service provision. The theories that follow are not just about UK school librarianship but are relevant to all sectors of the library profession in all parts of the world.

We will discuss these different discourses and their implications for us in the next section. To identify a discourse that is relevant to us begins a process of negotiation around the meaning of our role within the context of our workplace.

The discourses of professionalism

The language we use daily within our institutions is a reflection of the organization's accepted thinking. We use it to drive institutional policies and shape behaviour and responses. Such is the power of language that it creates a narrative that shapes our practice and identity. This is what we mean by discourse. On a larger scale discourse is a powerful tool used in the formation of policy by governments to solicit support and compliance. The study of discourse is mainly derived from the seminal work of the French philosopher Michel Foucault (1972). We can easily recognize its continuing significance in education where the use of language is always evolving to influence people's understanding and acceptance. For instance, 'remedial studies' of the 1960s and 1970s became 'special needs' in the 1980s and is now often referred to as 'learning support' (and, in the school library world, the 'school library' became a 'learning resource centre' or has evolved across the Atlantic to be a 'media resource center').

The discourse of managerialism

Typically the discourse of managerialism is externally imposed; it is not about individuals negotiating what they want to do. We may have some say in types of target-setting but generally this is done to other people's expectations. The discourse of managerialism emphasizes the manager's role in instilling accountability into the organization's culture. The discourse of managerialism is usually identified with the methods of the private sector that have been transferred to the public sector to encourage a culture of efficiency and economy. It aims to encourage conduct and activities that are considered appropriate in a market environment, as the market mechanism is considered to be the best driver of effectiveness. This is done by linking evaluation processes and performance review to value for money.

In education, the externally imposed demands are those of exam boards and publication of exam result league tables coupled with a system of inspection to monitor implementation. Knowledge of how we will be evaluated influences our behaviour, hence the pressure that teachers feel to 'teach to the test' rather than give attention to topics or skills that they might consider more appropriate for their students. School improvement plans could be seen as an outcome of the managerial discourse, as they allocate resources to desired changes, which are linked to central government priorities. Some of us may criticize this level of prescription and setting of common standards for reducing the level of autonomy available to teachers and librarians. Others see this as a method of achieving change for the better, in a manner that is rapid and cost-effective.

The managerialism of target-setting and the drive for cost-effectiveness can lead to tensions with the philosophies and ethics of librarianship. For example, public libraries in the UK are mainly measured by their issue statistics and therefore must tailor a large part of their stock to materials that are in high demand. On the surface this appears to be a sound business response. However, this can cause a tension with the public libraries' remit to support learning in the community. A traditional public library philosophy has been to fulfil the role of 'the people's university', but public libraries have been criticized for failing to develop the breadth and depth of their collections in the race to satisfy mainstream demands (Christie, 2008; Coates, 2013). Their approach to stock acquisition has also attracted criticism, when these processes have been contracted out to one major supplier for cost-efficiency reasons. It is possible that this has resulted in the purchase of materials of far less diversity than previously, leading to a neglect of smaller publishing houses and local bookselling businesses. Potentially this affects the quality and diversity of books published for all of us as the market adjusts to meet these big customer demands. Ethically, most librarians would avoid taking actions that are likely to be detrimental to the community and culture of the book trade. Librarians in large organizations are not responsible for all such decisions and pragmatism prevails in the face of managerialism.

If diversity of stock is contracting there is a conflict with the ethics of information provision and a greater danger of not meeting the needs of all parts of a community. Why should a service be valued by the whole community if it is not meeting the needs of all parts of that community?

The managerial model of school librarianship is one where we express effectiveness quantitatively, by value-added and other audit-measurable terms. This emphasizes the management skills of systems analysis, target-setting and evaluation. For the school librarian this may involve counting issues, reservations, catalogue use, student and class visits, and reporting on the size of collections and how they map to the curriculum. The following vignette demonstrates this approach.

The performance target of Alan, a school librarian, was to support a new module on the Tudors for A-level history. He provided publishers' catalogues for the teachers to select from and then purchased the items. A special subject heading was added to the online library catalogue so that pupils would be able to locate the selected books. Alan also used this heading to track the issue statistics. At the end of the year he produced a short report for the history department, which showed that very few resources had been borrowed.

In this example, Alan measured the library's effectiveness by assessing its system performance, just as when we measure a school's effectiveness only through its exam results, we know this tells us very little about the nature of the learning that takes place there. We may find in our schools that we have targets set for us to achieve, data that we are required to collect, but does that reflect what we really do?

The deputy head responsible for data analysis identified that those students with the highest number of classroom exclusions also had the weakest literacy levels. In order to improve their engagement with lessons she developed a holistic programme run by learning mentors. As part of that offer she asked the librarian to develop a reading project that would build the students' confidence and allow them to experience success as readers.

Clearly this deputy head's priorities, supported by the data, are to improve relationships and learning experiences for these students. Target-setting and number-crunching are tools and not necessarily ends in themselves. Even though we are operating under a managerial-style imposed target we can still reflect our philosophy of librarianship in our reporting. Do the data we report focus on teaching and learning through using resources, or only focus on the resources themselves?

If Alan in the earlier vignette had surveyed the history students to find out why their library usage was low, he might have obtained insights that would not surface through study of the systems data alone. Such an exercise could reveal barriers such as the lack of study space available in the library or a perception of the library not being a welcoming place, or simply that the history teachers never suggest that students use the library.

We can develop good practice as a result of personal learning and individuality rather than from an externally imposed set of standards or targets, as demonstrated in the following vignette.

Margaret was inspired by the master's programme she was studying, and developed an excellent library programme of activities as part of her school's chosen specialism: performing arts. A new deputy head teacher began to draw on Margaret's energy and resources to develop activities as part of initiatives to raise standards in spelling and grammar. Margaret had to re-prioritize her workload to meet these new demands. In addition to organizing the required spelling bee rounds across the school she also continued to provide poetry and writing competitions under the new banner of raising standards.

It is possible that imposing narrowly defined targets on Margaret might have stifled her creativity. In delivering work to meet the school's improvement goals, Margaret illustrates how management expertise enables the library to be tailored to the needs of its community, while enabling a librarian to remain inspired by their own values.

In an era of economic downturn schools are required to be evidence-based and accountable, and their teaching decisions informed by the data collected about student progress: the managerial model becomes dominant. There is less room to manoeuvre in this environment, and fewer opportunities for individual interpretation of role. Despite this it is still important to look at what professionalism means to us. By doing so we identify and articulate our underlying purpose and decide what we are not prepared to compromise on. This in itself confers a sense of personal autonomy. In times of adversity it is this sense of personal control and value that helps ensure our well-being and that is why professionalism remains important.

We need to consider how much time we spend on activities that fall within the managerial model. How far does the managerial model support the development of the library's educational role? Which of these activities, auditing the effectiveness of library systems or evaluating the educational role, would deliver the outcome most desired by the head teacher?

The discourse of technical rationalism

The discourse of technical rationalism characterizes professional activities as a set of solutions that can be applied to problems. Professional activities can be designated as competencies that can be broken down into their parts, as a set of skills that can be mastered and whose efficiency of delivery can be easily measured. Practitioners are accountable for the technical accuracy of their work. The model assumes that professionalism can be systematized as a set of guidelines and protocols, and that there is an equality of delivery. It does not make any allowance for the difference that varying levels of experience can make to the performance of a role.

When we apply this model to school librarianship we emphasize the mechanics of the role: cataloguing, issuing books, displaying work, sending lists of new books to teachers, organizing author talks and providing user education on how to use the library systems to locate items. The priority is to put the user in contact with the required item and at that point the librarian's responsibility in the process ends.

School librarian Diana delivered an induction lesson to Year 7 students every September. She gave each student a new library card and explained the rules of the library, its layout and the procedures for borrowing a book. She then gave students a worksheet to complete that enabled them to practise locating books using the Dewey Decimal Classification system. After some years Diana began talking more to other librarians, who suggested that she consider extending her role to include aspects that she had not previously considered. Diana realized that students had problems with defining what information they needed and in selecting useful search terms. She discussed her observations with teaching colleagues and realized it would be helpful to the students if she taught research skills as part of subject tasks, so they would learn in a more meaningful way at the point of need, rather than being expected to remember skills from a standalone context.

Some may be attracted by Diana's initial approach because it offers a clear definition of tasks. Alternatively, we may view the approach as reductionist, because it does not acknowledge the intellectual or creative processes involved in research. Some of us go further in our critique of the technical-rational discourse and view it as a denial of the complexity that fills real-life situations. In this stance, we see the intangible elements of intellect and creativity as essential parts of the professional expertise needed to lead a successful school library and so this discourse might be dangerously limited. It takes more than a set of technical skills to create a dynamic learning environment in a library that is vibrant and responsive to users' needs.

Making skills visible is a powerful imperative; if they are visible they are measurable and then, from an organizational point of view, manageable. From a professional association's point of view, if we make acquisition of a new skill visible, it can be rewarded. Continuing professional development is considered an inherent part of professionalism. We believe such development is more than just the acquisition of a new skill; it must also be an enrichment of understanding. New learning that leads to re-conceptualization is the most powerful form of continuing professional development. Should we as a professional view our practice as a series of problems to be solved or rather as a process requiring intellectual engagement to examine the different ways of fulfilling our role?

The narrative for this discourse does not acknowledge a professional identity motivated by an underlying purpose, fuelled with a set of values and philosophy. How visible are these values and the learning outcomes of the library? See Chapter 6 for a discussion of practice and impact.

The discourse of social democracy

This discourse of professionalism places an emphasis on the librarian's obligations to society, by maintaining justice and equality of access to library use for all. Its characteristics are those of collaborative leadership, shared decision making, and responsibility for processes and their outcomes, where professional judgements are valued.

In this discourse we emphasize opening dialogue with different stakeholders to aid in the designing and marketing of the service to appeal to all parts of the school community; this leads us quickly to the question of how to focus time and budget. In any school, it will not be possible to meet all of the needs all of the time, so targeting resources to achieve maximum effect is strategically vital. In some schools the librarian does this by putting energy into developing relationships with younger students, believing that this is a foundation for the students' time in the school. Others do it by prioritizing relationships with staff, hoping through working with them to reach many more students.

This discourse resonates with the inclusion agenda (Ofsted, 2014), which is promoted by central and local UK governments. The next vignette gives an example of considering the inclusion agenda when evaluating a library homework club.

Eliza decided to evaluate her library's homework club to find out what was most valued and least valued by its users and also to find out why some students never used it. A series of questionnaires and interviews yielded quantitative and qualitative data, answering not only the research question but revealing some unexpected results, too. This evidence helped managers plan future development and secure increased funding. An analysis was also made of the attendance register by age, ethnicity, ability banding and overlap with the special educational needs register. It concluded that the homework club appealed to all parts of the school's community and was therefore a successful part of the school's policy on inclusion. This evidence was then included in the school's self-evaluation prior to inspection.

Which comes first, the requirement to meet national targets or the desire to meet children's needs? The pragmatic librarian might argue that it does not have to be a choice; it is simply a matter of using the opportunities within national targets to help realize philosophical and ethical goals for the service. Others feel uncomfortable with the idea that they must find solutions to help society solve its social and economic needs as laid out in government targets. Can the social democratic librarian be all things to all people or must difficult choices be made?

School librarian Chris believed it was important to give students access to information about sex education including fiction featuring lesbian, gay, bisexual, trans and queer characters. The whole collection came under the spotlight when a parent complained that her child had borrowed a book which was unsuitable. The head teacher asked Chris to justify the inclusion of the book in the stock. Chris had to find a way to show respect for the parent's point of view, satisfy the head teacher's concern and maintain his view about the importance of giving students access to this collection.

We might also characterize the social democratic discourse as the view that librarians uphold when resisting censorship, whether generated by government, business corporations or individuals. Influenced by this discourse, the school librarian wants to make information accessible. At what point does duty of care towards students lead to censorship? Ethical dilemmas are at the heart of professional judgements; in examining our beliefs and reasons in relation to our role, how far will we defend them or how far will we go in order to realize them?

Student choice and his educational role are Nathan's two greatest influences when making decisions about the school library. He often experiences conflict: should he allow 11-year-old students to borrow only manga books or should he intervene believing that the reading skills of some students would benefit from also reading a text-based story? Should he negotiate with the students, setting them targets to widen their reading choices, offering the latest manga titles as part of the mix? Would this intervention be unethical?

The school librarian within this model acknowledges the importance of individual choice but in a school library this is also tempered by the educational aim of introducing students to the wider world of literature in all its forms. In educational terms, this social democratic model points towards the need for a learner-centred approach to working with students in the library environment.

The discourse of post-modernism

The post-modernist discourse in professionalism is seen as an expression of the uncertainty of roles and identities and a search for new ways of articulating the experience of living in a post-industrial, high-tech era of globalization. Post-modernist interpretations have both positive and negative visions for professionalism. Technology presents opportunities for professionals to create and communicate without boundaries. This can facilitate a revolt from what we may see as the more oppressive aspects of managerialism and technical rationalism.

Kai's line manager wished to review the school's extra-curricular offer, which involved counting the number of pupils entering the library at lunchtimes. Kai organized his library monitors to carry out the task but felt irritated as he thought they would not take account of the type of learning that took place in the library during a lunchtime. Conversations with an online librarian community allowed him to see that his role was being measured only in a technical sense, and the monitors did not reflect the education that takes place in this extra-curricular time. So instead of feeling de-professionalized he opened a conversation with his line manager and shared some examples of the learning taking place in the school library.

In response to the sense of threat to his status, Kai responded by exercising professionalism demonstrating a regard for the quality of his practice. Post-modernist interpretations also offer more pessimistic visions of professionalism. Within this discourse roles are seen as fragmented and de-professionalized by central control; their subjection to market values suggests that they no longer offer a meaningful personal sense of identity. The nature of professional identity is complex and it has been found that people experience phases of both stability and fragmentation at different times due to a variety of factors (Day et al, 2006). Professionalism is aptly defined as 'judgement in conditions of uncertainty' (Fish and De Cossart, 2006), which reflects the plural nature of our experiences. We make decisions, large or small, ethical or otherwise, amid the messiness that is real life.

Where does this leave school librarianship in the 21st century?

We are now in an age where universal truths are questioned. The digital world increasingly allows people to generate information and its free availability seems to have dispensed with the need for intermediaries to check content, either at the publication stage or at the point of access. Society's view of information is changing and in turn the role of the librarian is being questioned, not least by librarians themselves.

We can develop our vision of professionalism. We do not have to adopt a single type of discourse by which to measure ourselves; to do so may leave us confused, disempowered and de-professionalized. Discourses simply serve as a series of lenses through which to view our professionalism. It becomes more important than ever to examine our central values and to be clear about what we see as professional practice. There may be elements of each of these models that we need to meld and bring together into our vision. We need to be able to set targets, to be aware of skills required but also to move into the creative context. In education, the level of change we experience can be immense and the power of discourse is used in increasingly sophisticated ways. Having a clear personal vision enables us to identify when we are being re-positioned by a particular discourse and to engage with it critically, in order to achieve personal meaning, whether in agreement or disagreement.

Essential ingredients for success in this dynamic environment are a clear sense of self, vision and ethics. Even those who have been in the profession for some time recognize the need to re-examine values. Revisiting vision, ethics and values can help us identify the most appropriate course of action to take in the school. The word professionalism comes from the Latin word 'profiteor', to profess, to make a commitment to a set of values. It is this most intangible aspect of the concept that gives professionalism its greatest strength and passion. Naturally, implementing vision successfully must be underpinned by strategic thinking and this will be discussed in Chapters 5 and 6.

What is our view of professionalism in the school library? What should it encompass? If we want to raise our profile we need to develop a vision and articulate our underlying purpose: on which issues will we not compromise? What is it that we are prepared to fight for? Which tasks reflect the core values of our professionalism? That knowledge is the basis of our professionalism.

If our comfort zone lies within the model of technical rationalism but the school's leadership demands more of the activities associated with the social democratic model, the experience is not going to be easy. If the school's expectations are that we will simply stamp books and mind the space then those with social democratic leanings will feel unappreciated and become very frustrated.

In reality the successful school librarian is involved in a continuous negotiation of role, identity and professional values depending on the context of the situation. This is sometimes governed by our workplace and sometimes by our beliefs. Whether our priority is the day-to-day mechanics, teaching and learning or the nurturing of children, the outcomes from it will need to fit the school's vision in order to be considered effective. Once we have a grasp of our own model it is time to focus on how others see us.

In Chapter 2 we look at how other people see us, enabling us to explore the congruence, or lack of it, between those perspectives and our own.

How others see us

Regardless of how we view ourselves as professionals, we work within the context of other people's perceptions of us and demands on us. While the library may be referred to by some (e.g. Libraries All Party Parliamentary Group, 2014) as the 'heart of the school' this does not mean that it is always, in practice, central to school life. Indeed, some people may see the librarian as peripheral to the teaching and learning 'business' of the school. Even where the library is positioned physically at the middle or the front of the school building, as is certainly the case in some schools, we need to recognize that this is only part of what being central means. Far more important is the library's relationship to the curriculum and the extent to which the librarian is included in the planning and delivery of teaching and learning in all its manifestations. In this chapter we will discuss how different groups regard this relationship and the effect this has on what the librarian can achieve.

People within the school community
Head teachers

Head teachers determine how the school's resources are to be distributed, subject only to the governors' approval, and their vision of education has an enormous impact on our role. Ofsted (2006) underlined the importance of head teachers in setting the school library context:

> Leadership by supportive and knowledgeable headteachers and senior managers was the most important factor in improving library provision. They recognized how libraries contributed to learning and, wherever possible, they appointed specialist librarians to lead developments.
>
> Overwhelmingly, the most significant element in bringing about improvements was the commitment and support of effective head teachers.

A survey of head teachers' attitudes to the school library, commissioned by the UK All Party Parliamentary Group for Libraries, published in 2014, found that well over 90% of those who responded valued their school libraries. Given this enthusiasm, why do so many schools not have a professionally staffed school library? Lack of head teacher support may not be the only reason, but given how crucial this support is for the development of an effective school library there are obviously many who remain unconvinced about the school library's contribution to student learning and do not support it. There is no doubt that the advent of a new head teacher is a nervous time for any school, but there have been sufficient instances of new head teachers simply dismissing the value of the librarian (and even the library) and making it impossible to operate, for the librarian to feel particularly vulnerable. On the other hand, a head teacher with a positive view can create a climate within a school whereby the librarian is expected to be involved at all levels of curriculum planning and delivery. Such a head teacher may empower the librarian to lead or collaborate in a variety of areas, such as on the school's literacy work or the programme for the more able students, or in developing information literacy throughout the curriculum.

Tom is a creative, qualified and experienced librarian with a passion for information literacy. He was delighted when he secured a job in a school where the head teacher was as enthusiastic as he was about collaborating with subject teachers to embed these skills within the curriculum. Tom enjoyed teacher status and made full use of this, taking classes and being responsible for the assessment of work. The measurable results he achieved were noted by teachers and the head teacher as contributing to the success of the school. To Tom's dismay the head teacher left and the successor had a very different vision of how the library should be run. Tom was placed under pressure to remain at the library desk at all times through the loss of the library assistant post. These constraints on any possible work with classes made Tom frustrated that his professional expertise was no longer being maximized. He felt he had no option but to leave and pursue his career elsewhere. He was saddened and shocked by this sudden change.

Teachers

In the 1990s Streatfield and Markless (1994) found that the single most important factor leading to effective use of libraries in primary and secondary schools was a positive attitude by teachers. Today's school librarians still rely heavily on teachers' willingness to co-operate with them. College and university students spend a lot of their time working independently but the school day for students up to age 16 is usually taken up with taught lessons. Therefore school librarians only become part of the learning process with the approval, support and collaboration of teaching colleagues. School librarians depend on teachers seeing a role for us in developing the learning of their students and being prepared to work closely with us as partners. In recent doctoral research Webb (2013) found that, through the lens of their subject, teachers have a specific view of the role played by information in teaching. It follows, therefore, that they each view the librarian's role differently. So we must ensure that we understand differing subject approaches in order to tailor what we offer in each area. When teachers and curriculum time are under so much pressure because they are judged by test results above all else, how can we expect teachers to be receptive to someone who seems to add to the complexity of teaching?

Students

Students are another significant group whose perceptions shape our role. How they respond to us will affect our services. The fact that much of what we do is delivered straight to students as individuals, rather than mediated through the teachers, may give us value in their eyes, and enable us to have a real impact. Perversely, the work that we do that is not channelled directly via a teacher may diminish its value to some students. Whatever our impact, it is seldom articulated by the students, and is difficult to measure. They may even see it as personal to them as individuals rather than as part of the educational process. When 'student voice' is a significant part of the way a school is judged, it is important that we seize the opportunity to access and affect student opinion.

When a new head teacher was appointed at school librarian Nadira's school, she was surprised that the library was not on his itinerary during the familiarization days he spent at the school before taking up his post. She was keen to hear his vision for a school library but found no opportunity to discuss this with him during his first term. Later she heard through her line manager that he wanted the library to be a more vibrant place and a hub of activity. She discovered that he built his picture of the library through speaking to students in all year groups and listening to their opinions and experiences.

Here we see that a head teacher formed his opinion not through direct experience of the library, but by listening to students. While we may feel that it would have been helpful to have spoken directly to the librarian, it is clear that this head teacher saw the students' perception of the library as paramount. Heads and senior managers will pay attention to what students are saying and thinking, so librarians need to pay equal attention and to be aware of how students feel about the library. How can we use their wishes to enhance the service we offer them most effectively? How do we access their opinions in our schools? And how do we go beyond speaking merely to a subset or subsets of the student body, to reaching out to them all?

Governors

Governors representing the local community may determine the level of budget and other resources we are given to work with. Their decisions will depend on how they perceive the role of school librarians. Some will have well developed views about this, perhaps resulting from their own or their children's experiences; others may have less fixed views. In either case, governors may be influenced by the attitudes of senior leaders who they meet. If they see the librarian mentioned in an inspection report or featured in the school's self-evaluation form, or if they are invited to be involved in a librarian's appointment, their expectations of the role of the librarian may be enhanced. How can we be sure that information about what we are doing and its effectiveness reaches them?

Governors in each school approach their roles slightly differently, so it is necessary to find out how they operate in our individual schools. How are staff represented on the governing body? How can we feed information either to those members of staff or directly to governors? How do we develop governors' sense of the library's value, particularly in preparation for critical decisions, such as the appointment of a new head, or indeed in preparation for our own replacement?

Parents

Many parents who are looking round schools with a view to deciding where to send their children seem genuinely concerned about the service the library can offer. CILIP's School Libraries Group recognized this as an opportunity to get our message across and published a leaflet in 2013 aimed at advising parents about what to look for in a school library. The image that the concerned parent may have of an effective library may be quite different from the one librarians have. Can parents directly influence how the school librarian is perceived? Do we even want them to? If we do desire this, how do we achieve it? Do we want them to look at basic issues such as resources and staffing, or do we want to raise their awareness of the services we wish to offer and the educational value we bring to the students?

Teachers frequently meet parents at events such as formal academic review days but there may be little direct contact between librarian and parent. We should be proactive in engaging with them, for example by participating at such events, issuing reading and book lists, or taking part in parent workshops. In our experience, the informal involvement of parents in the library is expanding. Themed events, cross-curricular days and author visits need to be planned to reach out to include parents. Some parents may also make direct contact and prompt the librarian to develop initiatives such as homework guidelines.

We need to know what the parents of our school want, as well as looking at whether we can develop services that will enhance their view of what we are doing for their children's education. We might solicit support from parent–teacher associations, or use contact with parent governors to clarify what would be useful and valued.

Within independent schools the views of parents may have an even larger role in the way the school presents the library. Such schools are businesses as well as educational bodies, and attracting parent customers is crucial to their existence. Those not directly involved in educational roles may hark back to their schooldays to form views on what is important. This can put a greater premium on the traditional image of the library than we might wish: silent, studious and book-dominated.

Frances was appointed as the librarian in an independent co-educational boarding school to run a newly refurbished library. The head was very proud of her new facility since it was her last major project before her retirement, and she took every opportunity to promote the library to prospective parents. A survey conducted by the school's marketing department confirmed that after a year the library had a significant positive impact on parental choice in a competitive market. However, Frances noticed that student use of the library was declining. She conducted a survey, which confirmed her suspicions, and suggested to senior management that the stock should be changed and rearranged to reflect better the needs of the students, even though this would lead to an obvious change in the rather austere traditional environment. Her request was denied because the senior teachers believed it would detract from what parents would expect to see. Frances made some small changes and eventually an inspection report referred to 'a well stocked, well managed but poorly used library'. At the same time, another independent school had hit the headlines with its very different approach to library provision. This gave Frances the necessary ammunition to ask again to change and rearrange the stock, and this time her suggestions were given serious thought and many were accepted and acted on.

Here we see how traditional attitudes to the library and other outside influences may exert surprising pressure on what may or may not drive changes within the school library.

Bodies outside the school
Government and national bodies

The independent sector aside, the level of resources that we receive can be determined by views within local and central government, through the overall budgets given to schools. More importantly, the views of members of government and national bodies can make a significant difference to how school librarians are perceived within the school and community, through reports these people commission, comments they make and their visits to schools, with the accompanying profile that brings. External advisers and inspectors may have an influence on both government itself and the public pressures on government to act in particular ways. National bodies such as (in the UK) the Reading Agency and the National Literacy Trust may highlight or downplay the role of the school library. National and international research may also influence policy directly or indirectly by feeding into the political discourse. Finally, international reports, such as the Programme for International Student Assessment (PISA) reports, comparing UK educational achievements with those of other countries, may influence the political and educational environments.

What influences how others see us and how can we influence their perceptions?
How we see and present ourselves

The activities that we prioritize and where we focus our resources and efforts affect the way others see us, and whether they view us as fellow educationalists. If we behave like clerks and the most visible thing we do is send out overdue notices then we will be seen as administrators and treated as such. So, as Stenhouse (1975) advocated more than 40 years ago, we need to move from operating largely within the technical-rational role, to developing into 'consultative tutors' able to support students' independent learning. In this era of personalized learning plans and the monitoring of every student to show progress, this may at last be a realistic role for school librarians. This belief in the value of the librarian can be generated by school librarians themselves. Indeed, given the pressures on their time and energy, it is likely that many teachers will need the active example of an effective and creative librarian to be able to develop this belief and act on it.

Paul was facing the prospect of his library being largely replaced by electronic resources. He set out to demonstrate that he could work to the head's educational agenda, which prioritized students' competence and confidence in the electronic environment, linked to employability. He pointed out that digital literacy skills such as website evaluation and internet searching are no longer being taught because information and communication technology (ICT) has been removed from the National Curriculum in England, and proposed that he, as the 'information expert', should fill this gap. He became fundamental to the vision of the school's development by collaborating with teachers, in the classroom and in the library, to ensure that students were able to obtain and use information in all its formats effectively.

By publicly embracing the changes that have happened and are still happening in the supply and flow of information, we can position ourselves more securely, not as gatekeepers but as facilitators and enablers, opening students' eyes to the realities of using information effectively. Information literacy skills are morphing into digital literacy skills. We need to show that our skills are central to developing students' skills – not just in handling information but in generating it creatively and intellectually. However, we can only do this if we have the confidence in our position and the self-esteem to make us push ourselves forward.

Our position in school

Our position in the school hierarchy and employment status can make all the difference to what we can achieve. It determines how the school community regards us and may limit or expand how we operate.

The line management of the librarian can have a huge impact on their role and status. CILIP (Shaper, 2014) recommends that 'the librarian is line managed by a senior leadership team member with responsibility for curriculum development'. If school librarians are line managed within the same structure as teachers, they will be included in academic decision making. However, if line management is outside the main curriculum structure school librarians may be seen as separate from teaching and learning. Being marginalized in this way makes it very difficult for our professional expertise to be seen and used fully, as demonstrated in the following vignette.

Jennifer had worked in the school for some time and had been line managed by a deputy head. A reorganization of the support staff resulted in her being placed within the administrative team. She was now line managed by the bursar. The change left Jennifer separated from the academic staff and she found it difficult to carry out effective liaison with teachers and keep up to date with current teaching and learning issues within the school. It also became increasing difficult as each attempt to align herself with teachers seemed like an affront to her new 'team'. As a result, in spite of a number of attempts to make the new system work, Jennifer eventually decided that the situation was untenable and resigned.

Such situations are so complex that outcomes are never simple; line managers may not have the understanding or authority to alter the position. Indeed, they may not have the inclination to help for political reasons of their own. Dealing with this type of conflict is discussed in Chapter 3 but, like Jennifer, we have to accept that in some circumstances we will not be able to change how others see us.

Fortunately, not all librarians are line managed in the way described in the vignette about Jennifer. A post by a deputy head on the School Librarians' Network (an e-mail group with over 1300 members, founded in 1998 for people interested in school libraries) in 2008 showed a very different attitude to the librarian and his role in the school's decision-making processes:

> In summary, our librarian is precise, accurate, efficient and all-encompassing in his approach. This is simply what a good librarian is. However, he is also insightful, creative in his approaches – he often uses phrases like 'let's turn this problem on its head' to find the solution – helpful (even at cost to himself) and never ever allows his personal opinion to colour anything he does. He is at the heart of the school and this is often reflected by his magnetic effect on those students who would not normally be expected to be seen in a library.
>
> Is he troublesome? He certainly is!! Due to the fact that he sets extremely high standards for his own work and outcomes, he builds a framework which allows others to meet those high standards and, naturally, expects them to be met. When they are not, he does not accept this and move on; he asks those questions – why did this not happen? What can I do to allow it to happen? How can we make it better? Life is easier without tenacity like that – but of lower quality!

Clearly, the librarian built this attitude through his own activities; equally clearly, the school recognized his value and exploited it fully.

With the expansion of senior leadership teams and a multiplicity of responsibility points for different interventions, there is often less time for line managers to nurture people and less time available for librarians to communicate with senior leadership teams to cultivate understanding of what it takes to make a library run well. This further underlines the need for us to communicate documentary evidence about the success of our role to the line manager, rather than relying on conversations.

Where the line-management structure leads teachers to recognize us as equals, this is likely to shape student opinion. Actions and attitudes that they see in others around them, especially adults in school and at home, will influence teachers' behaviour and their expectations. When librarians are not respected ambivalence creeps in and students are unsure of our status and authority. For example, if teachers do not assess information skills, or do not allow us to, students will not see the value of our expertise.

Teachers' recognition of the librarian's authority is crucial but so, too, is our willingness to assume that authority.

Similarly, parents will follow the school's lead in how they regard the librarian and so we must consider how we appear on the school's website or prospectus. Are our qualifications listed alongside those of the teachers? If the staffing structure is shown, are we placed among the academic staff? We should ensure that we post news items as other heads of department do. We also need to consider carefully how we communicate with parents in other ways such as by giving advice about reading or assessments.

Media and public opinion

The media picture of librarians remains dubious, stuck in a past of buns and twin-sets, fingers to lips and stamping out books. The headline of a relatively recent article in praise of libraries included the phrase 'Get the old grumpy librarians out' (Paquet, 2014). We need to dispel this image and demonstrate that, amid a rising tide of information, we enable students and staff to grasp the critical literacies they need. We need to show that we use learning technologies and innovative software to communicate with and stimulate our users. In short, the media representation of us is quite simply wrong.

Unfortunately for us those in the media tend to use outdated stereotypes of public librarians to drive their portrayal of the whole profession. They 'overlook' the professional aspects of the public library role, which are often hidden behind a layer of non-professional library managers and assistants. Although we are supposed to live in an 'information' or 'knowledge' society, this has not enhanced our role as information professionals; there is often a failure to recognize that a plethora of information creates the same need for support as a dearth of information. The apparent availability of information to anyone with an internet connection seems to have convinced many that access has been achieved. In fact, we know that only a tiny percentage of information is freely available on the internet since much is hidden from the general public in academic or commercial databases, and without good digital literacy skills people often struggle to find good information, or to know when they have failed to do so. How can we show that true access depends on the ability to assess accuracy, bias, reliability, comprehensibility and relevance? Is physical access being confused with intellectual access?

Finally, we have to face up to the fact that many people think that the need for a school library is so obvious that it does not need to be stated and, all too often, they are incredulous when they come across a school that has no library. It is up to us all to keep the message in the public eye by generating news items in the press and using social media such as blogs and Twitter to raise public awareness of school librarianship at its best. Equally important, though more problematic politically, is highlighting when posts are axed or libraries closed.

Evidence

A very real problem for UK school librarians has been the lack of evidence about the impact of their work. This in turn has a negative influence on the willingness of UK politicians to direct scarce resources to us. Research elsewhere, notably in the USA, suggests that there is a direct correlation between academic success and the active presence of well qualified library staff. The instigator of much of this research, Keith Curry Lance, writes: 'A central finding of this study is the importance of a collaborative approach to information literacy' (Lance, Rodney and Hamilton-Pennell, 2000). We need to publicize such evidence that students do better with guidance from actively involved librarians. To do this, we need to develop national evidence of our effectiveness and combine this with international evidence; then we need to find ways of communicating this evidence to the decision makers.

The report *School Libraries in the UK* (Streatfield, Shaper and Rae-Scott, 2010), the All Party Parliamentary Group report mentioned above (Libraries All Party Parliamentary Group, 2014) and the Scottish report on the impact of school libraries on learning (Williams, Wavell and Morrison, 2013) have started to build an evidence base. It is however clear that at present the onus remains on individual professionals to evaluate our work and make it visible to the outside world.

Another influence on the attitudes of teachers is the inspection process. People will naturally work to the criteria on which they will be evaluated. Hence, an inspection or (in the UK) the school's self-evaluation form can be very significant. It is easy for us to see that we can feed naturally into the self-evaluation process, as is shown in Appendix 2 at the end of the book. Equally, it is easy to see how the library can be omitted from the self-evaluation form by schools with no recognition of the library's value, and if we are not sufficiently proactive this will happen.

School libraries in the UK have had a rather mixed experience of school inspections. Under the older, longer inspections, inspectors frequently spent time inspecting the library, even if the actual report gave little space to it. Under the later shorter inspections, when specific targets have been chosen before visiting a school, far less attention is given to libraries. Where libraries have been mentioned in inspection reports it is because the librarian has provided evidence of their impact on an aspect of teaching and learning. How to generate such evidence will be looked at in Chapter 6.

What are the implications of others' perceptions of the librarian?

The most obvious consequence of how others see us is the employment or not of school librarians. Though the latest UK National Curriculum framework (Department for Education, 2014b) states that all maintained schools should provide library facilities we regularly hear of professional librarians being made redundant or having hours cut. If expectations are limited, then the vision is likely also to be limited, with many school managers believing that it is adequate to employ unqualified and therefore cheaper staff to fulfil those expectations.

Many UK school librarians are appointed part-time, and as a result until recently they may have been seen as less committed professionals. Perhaps fortunately for us, part-time working is becoming more common within the teaching profession and so the image of part-timers has improved. However, one worrying recent trend in the face of serious budget cuts has been the increasing alteration of librarians' terms and conditions to term-time only. This has huge implications for the recruitment and retention of high quality professionals and the morale of the profession. It certainly places limitations on what can be achieved.

Nevertheless, so long as school librarians believe that what we do matters to our students, we are professionally obliged to do the most we can to make ourselves count within the school community and beyond: within the community, because that is where we work, and beyond it, so that our effectiveness may build a deeper understanding of school librarianship and challenge the wider education community to exploit that role. Whatever the perceptions, librarians need to operate both within them, by taking them into account in what we do, and beyond them, by pushing at the boundaries of others' ideas to create new areas where we can work and develop our sphere of influence. The reality of this way of working is explored in the next chapter.

Bridging the gap between how we see ourselves and how others see us

A gap between practice and professional beliefs can arise in all sectors of the library world and, it appears, in all areas of education. Indeed, some experienced teachers are finding that the ideals that attracted them to the profession are no longer valued and that priorities they do not share rule the day. Cognitive dissonance is a term that describes what happens when someone has to absorb opposing points of view (Festinger, 1957) or when new information or a new interpretation of information challenges existing knowledge or ideals (Atherton, 2013). We may experience this when our vision differs from that of our school community. What may seem the 'professional pathway' for us may conflict with the school leadership's plans. When this happens, a dichotomy may arise between principles and practice and we will need to bridge the gap between others' expectations and our beliefs.

Is there always a dichotomy between principles and practice?

What level of congruence between our own ideology and our school's requirements should we expect? We frequently reconcile ourselves to the fact that not everything can be ideal and we will not always be in total sympathy with our employers. Unfortunately, as time goes by, tensions may develop when we are constrained to act against our values, in order to comply with the school's outlook, and so a gulf between belief and practice may emerge. The cognitive dissonance we experience may cause a gradual modification in our views as a result of accommodating to the school's required behaviour. On the other hand, a confident practitioner might take a job exactly because of that challenge, because it offers the opportunity for them to make a real difference. Influence and impact can work both ways in reconciling opposing views.

Sometimes we do not have access to the vision and strategy of our senior leaders and instead we are on the receiving end of operational necessities. If we do not understand the bigger picture it is easy to perceive a conflict between our own ideas and those of the leadership team. In our turn, we may not take steps to communicate our vision of the library and where it sits in the work of the school. We need to understand what is going on and not necessarily characterize it as a gap.

James established his secondary school library as a zoned space with each area designated for a different purpose. This included an area of tables set aside for 'silent working'. James worked hard to get this respected by his students but was regularly frustrated by teachers who ignored the policy when they were looking for somewhere quiet to interview a pupil. It was easy to take their behaviour as a personal affront but after talking to a trusted colleague he realized that the teachers were not intentionally undermining him but were just acting in the heat of the moment. James decided that his colleagues were usually very supportive and so he would not allow this one thing to cause him stress.

James realized that this was not a dichotomy between beliefs and practice but just teachers doing what was expedient. Dealing with this sort of behaviour can be tiring and awkward and, of course, each time there is a new member of staff the issue of how to use the library space may need to be revisited, but it is not really a clash of philosophy.

In what circumstances might a dichotomy between beliefs and practice occur?

Misunderstandings at appointment can lead to disagreements surfacing fairly quickly. Sometimes a potential dichotomy between beliefs and practice is not anticipated because certain assumptions have been made at interview, or the expectations of the role have not been made clear. The following vignettes illustrate how misconceptions can arise on both sides.

A vacancy arose at an independent school for a librarian, reporting to the finance manager. The previous post-holder had been a dual-qualified teacher librarian, had taught information literacy throughout the school and was a member of the academic staff. Iram had worked previously in public libraries and was offered the position as a member of the support staff, which she gladly accepted, midway through the summer term. It was a surprise when in September she was asked to conduct library lessons. She refused, stating that she was appointed to a non-teaching post to run the library and no mention had been made of taking classes when she had applied for the job. It was not something she wished to do.

The contradiction between beliefs and practice may not be between the librarian and the school but due to external pressures, as seen in the next scenario.

Judith's family circumstances had changed and she decided a spell abroad might give her a fresh start. She was appointed as a Chartered librarian at an international school in the Middle East. She had many years' experience of running school libraries but nothing had prepared her for the isolation, censorship and restriction to outside information that she encountered. Although her new employers were liberal, the confines imposed by the country in which she was working made it difficult for Judith to resource the library and engage the students according to her professional values. There was no public library system to help provide resources, few other librarians to consult, and she had to contend with websites being banned at national level and censorship of some images.

Whether the dichotomy between beliefs and practice is due to misconceptions or external factors it is usually catalytic in nature leading to changes in understanding or circumstances.

In reality, a dichotomy between beliefs and practice is most likely to surface when there are changes in the school, for example, the appointment of a new head teacher or line manager, the school needs to respond to an external inspection report, or there is a reduction in funding levels. Libraries can be an easy target for a new leader trying to make an impression, because they tend to be more public than other areas of the school and are visible to parents and governors as well as students and teachers. When expectations are suddenly changed, and the outlook for the library changes, we may view the new circumstances with unease and insecurity rather than as a welcome challenge. The librarian described in the vignette below faced such a dilemma.

Amy was delighted when the new head teacher of a rural comprehensive school in which she worked announced that she had big plans for the library. To Amy's dismay, it emerged that the head teacher's idea was to turn the space into a classroom and to merge the library with the IT centre because she felt that books had 'had their day' and she wanted a more modern, hi-tech image for her school. The head teacher also suggested that the IT manager rather than the deputy head could be Amy's line manager.

It takes negotiation skills, confidence and allies for someone to accept changes like this and work out a compromise, and sometimes the changes lead to a battle that is just not going to be won. Regarding it as an opportunity rather than a threat demands of Amy that she changes her vision for the library. Maybe, with extra training and careful people management, the school will achieve an amicable outcome for everyone but perhaps Amy will feel so undermined and undervalued that she has to move on.

External influences can be positive. School inspections may criticize poor library provision and be a catalyst for improvements. However, the quirks of government policy can lead to unforeseen difficulties. For example, many school librarians have embodied values of encouraging students' independence, inclusion and allowing them space to engage with resources without having to meet particular learning targets. When government policy in the UK made judging schools by the progress of particular identified groups a priority many schools responded by increasing support for those targeted students during and beyond the school day. This stifled their freedom of choice in how they use the library.

We have examined some sources of tension that are tangible and specific. However, cognitive dissonance is not always a conscious experience. Underlying tensions may build up over time, fed by isolation and insecurity. We may expect to be seen as making an important contribution to teaching and learning but find ourselves regarded as an administrator and 'warehouse manager'. In this situation, our belief about our role may conflict with what seems to be required by the school. It is easy to believe that we have no input into the school's decision-making processes and become frustrated or disconsolate.

Graham was particularly annoyed when he put forward proposals for author visits to his senior leadership team and received little or no response. Finally he spoke to his line manager, one of the deputy head teachers, about his frustration over the lack of support in organizing outside speakers for the students. She explained that they were not keen on such visits because they had previously had a bad experience and felt that there were not enough controls over what a speaker might say to their students. She felt their duty of care outweighed the unknown value that such a talk might give students. When Graham overcame his shock at this explanation, he realized that he thought this represented a form of censorship. If they would not allow authors onto the premises, might certain books be next for exclusion? He felt that to pursue what he considered valuable in encouraging a healthy reading culture would only result in further marginalization by the leadership team. He gave serious consideration to accepting the status quo and simply complying with this ethos, but ultimately the strain placed on his professional beliefs led him to seek new employment.

The lack of dialogue between Graham and his senior leadership team caused a deterioration in the situation described above. The team's misconceptions about the role of the librarian as a professional led them to dismiss Graham's possible contribution to a healthy reading culture. If they had given Graham the opportunity to voice his concerns and had shown more respect for his judgement, then Graham might not have felt so victimized and the outcome might have been more positive for everyone. Perhaps Graham could have provided evidence for his views on how to develop a healthy reading culture and shown references from other schools to reassure management about the quality and suitability of the authors he was proposing.

So, we can see that dichotomies arise in many situations. It can happen when we see things in a fundamentally different way from others in our community. We may regard ourselves as having an educational role in promoting information literacy but our school wants an administrator to run their library. We might want to promote the power of written literature but our school managers may believe the internet is all that is necessary. Our school's senior leadership team may demand a silent, austere study space but we might desire a modern, social library. We may see great potential and have ideas for the development of our library but the funding committee might have other priorities.

Awareness of potential dichotomies between beliefs and practice may also come from insights into what is thought to be best practice by others in the world of education. Why do we consider the work of others, or read a set of standards such as those produced for school libraries by the International Federation of Library Associations (IFLA, 2006) if not to examine our performance? IFLA's concepts of 'cultural sensitivity' and 'intellectual access' are deeply thought provoking. For instance, how do we balance our duty of care to under-age students against the need to provide information about their health? Is this duty of care a real concept or our way of avoiding providing material that might be considered controversial?

A thought-provoking article or conference presentation can cause us to examine the principles of our professional philosophy. Intellectually we may agree to follow a code of ethics which we do not question, such as those regarding copyright issues. However, codes of ethics are, by their very nature, limited in their reach and in many areas we may find a gulf. Detecting these divergences and seeking resolution helps us to understand why we do what we do, and is part of developing a professional identity. It can be tempting when unavoidable tension arises to bury our own values. However, in the long run, this is not necessarily a healthy response for us or our school. Is avoiding confrontation the best way forward?

How can we resolve the dichotomy between beliefs and practice?

Developing awareness of the world in which we operate, as discussed in Chapters 1 and 2, is our first step. Dialogue with the wider profession helps us to examine the experience of dichotomy between principles and practice in our working life. Isolation clouds our understanding and contact with other librarians helps us to be more objective. This understanding gives us choices for possible resolutions.

Certainly, when we apply for any new job it is advisable to examine the vision the school has for its library and to see how closely this matches our own ideals. We need to ask ourselves 'will I feel valued by this employer?' Conflict may be avoided if the school has a clear vision of what it wants and produces a job description in line with that vision. The values and outlook of a school should be evident to the prospective librarians at the staff selection interview, so that candidates can judge for themselves whether a dichotomy between beliefs and practice is likely to arise and whether they wish to continue with their application. For example, a librarian with a passion for reading who applies for a job in a technical college where most of the students are pursuing practical vocational qualifications might expect to encounter a resistance to the introduction of schemes for promoting wider reading. This potential mismatch needs to be explored before an appointment is made or a position accepted. Would the librarian's survival instinct and self-awareness allow them to adapt and grow or would the change be too much for their mindset to accommodate? At interviews we answer many questions but it is also really important to establish what the post entails and the line-management structure by asking searching questions. We must do our homework and not be afraid to say no if we feel uncomfortable. To find ourselves in a job where there is a serious mismatch between personal vision and the school's viewpoint will be frustrating and possibly demoralizing. The employer, too, should be seeking the best possible match and should re-advertise the post if necessary.

Kirsty attended an interview at a boys' independent school along with three other applicants. She was a very experienced, well qualified school librarian. The physical appearance of the library was old-fashioned and during the course of the interview it became apparent that so were the views of the senior leadership team. Kirsty felt that to make the changes she believed would be needed would require a lot of determination and could well meet with resistance. She knew she would not be content just to adjust to the status quo. Halfway through the interview she withdrew her application. The post was subsequently offered to another candidate.

Kirsty was explicitly aware of a potential dichotomy between her views and those of her interviewing panel so she was able to make an informed decision. However, not everyone can afford to worry about whether an organization's view fits in with their professional philosophy before accepting a job. Our financial or personal circumstances may not allow us to have the luxury of choice. In taking on a post in the knowledge that there are potential conflicts we must be prepared to adjust our expectations. This is the day-to-day reality for many of us.

That reality, when experienced in what is a very demanding and busy work environment, can be stressful. It is important to keep stress levels manageable, not only for the sake of our personal well-being but also to keep our performance effective. One way to ensure this happens is to develop clear communication channels. How can we be effective in the eyes of an employer if we are not aware of what effectiveness looks like to them? An appraisal system is a useful tool for clarifying work objectives and how they determine day-to-day tasks. It enables expectations to be examined, feedback exchanged and targets set that fit in with the school vision. The effectiveness of any organization increases when there are high levels of trust in the relationships between staff. Therefore communications need to be open and we and our line managers need to feel listened to and valued. Where there is no open communication between staff, dissatisfaction increases and can result in high levels of absence, a larger turnover of staff and an atmosphere of conflict.

It takes confidence to negotiate with this reality and a determination to focus on issues rather than personalities. A useful source of support and strategies for developing good workplace relationships in the UK is the Advice, Conciliation and Arbitration Service (www.acas.org.uk) and there are broadly equivalent organizations offering help in resolving conflict in some other countries. Human resources and personnel management organizations (such as the Chartered Institute of Personnel and Development in the UK; www.cipd.co.uk) have many resources and may provide models of good practice and effective management.

We all have to make compromises from time to time and we have to be flexible in order to survive. The big question is when is it acceptable to give way on an issue? When is something so important to our personal vision that it is a fundamental principle not to be compromised? Many school librarians are solo professionals, and it can be particularly hard for them to make this judgement because there may be no one with whom to discuss any particular problem. In isolation and under pressure, it is easy to lose a sense of perspective and matters can become very personal. We should remember that senior staff have a duty of care for their team members, and trades union representatives may also be sources of support and advice. Relationships with other librarians in similar positions are more than useful; they are an essential lifeline for support in any difficult situation. Discussion with others who have faced similar difficulties can bring new perspectives and understanding, ideas for ways forward, or simply support in doing what must be done.

Indeed the process may well result in a re-examination of attitudes that are to the benefit of one's professional practice, as can be seen in the next vignette. What would have happened if Amy, from the earlier vignette, had reacted differently?

Amy was delighted when the new head teacher of a rural comprehensive school announced that she had big plans for the library. To Amy's dismay, it emerged that her plan was to turn the space into a classroom and to merge the library with the IT centre because she felt that books had 'had their day' and she wanted a more modern hi-tech image for her school. The head teacher suggested that the IT manager rather than the deputy head could be Amy's line manager. Amy visited another school to see this vision in operation and came back with ideas of how to reconcile her own priorities with the new plan. She put together a proposal regarding the introduction of e-books and online resources and requested a meeting to discuss team-teaching opportunities to develop pupils' use of these resources.
Meanwhile, she worked with departments to assess the needs for continued provision in other formats including newspapers, magazines and fiction texts for the less able and in foreign languages.

The emotions first experienced were deeply unhappy and uncomfortable ones, but Amy did not over-react to them and instead took time to consider and research what such a change really represented and how it could be managed. By reflecting on the head teacher's priority Amy has found a way forward that maintains what she believes to be an important core service but also supports the overall school goal. Sometimes it is only when we are challenged to move out of our comfort zones that moments of real learning and understanding occur and that can be fundamental to how we see our role.

We began this chapter by defining what we mean by dichotomy and we have examined various manifestations in school librarianship. Although resolutions of any particular issue are not always possible, the symptoms can be alleviated through deeper understanding of the problems, by careful reflection and perhaps in discussion with others. We can then articulate our point of view more clearly and enhance our professional practice. If the level of dissonance is too uncomfortable and progress towards a resolution unlikely, then we have to decide whether to move on. Total congruence between our principles and practice is never likely to be achieved but an acceptable level of compromise can make things workable.

PART 2

YOUR COMMUNITY: FROM PERCEPTIONS TO PRACTICE

CHAPTER 4

Identifying and understanding your community

Throughout this book a key message has emerged: the librarian who is closely identified with the processes of teaching and learning within the school has the power to make the most difference. Understanding our community and the range of opportunities there is crucial if we are to make this a reality. This is not as easy as it might first appear. Schools are highly complex organizations and political in nature – and things are not always as they appear. Exploring beneath the surface will help us to ascertain the teaching and learning priorities of the school so that we can focus our energies. Ultimately our research informs our management of change and leadership of learning.

How do we define our community?

We have to be clear about how we see our school community. Since it consists of individuals whose needs are ever changing as they grow and develop, study of these needs enables us to evaluate our effectiveness in developing the library's role. Our professional ethics require us to ensure that our services are representative and inclusive of all in that community, but in practical terms we have to decide who we think the library is for. Should we buy popular adult fiction for staff holiday reads? Should we buy books in Russian for just one pupil when Russian is not on the curriculum? Should we lend materials to the local primary school? Should we provide a collection of resources for school governors?

There is also the wider community of parents and governors. Do we see provision for these groups as part of our role? In the UK, schools in the independent sector must develop their role of charitable use, and in the state sector schools are under pressure to extend their opening hours and enhance community involvement. Do we need to think about who will use our services beyond the school walls and if so how do we respond to this responsibility? Recent technological advances and the use of social media have made it easier to share information with others.

We also need to address the issues surrounding diversity and discrimination within our community. The Equality Act 2010 consolidates and simplifies discrimination law. Advice from the Department for Education about this act summarizes a key point: 'Schools cannot unlawfully discriminate against pupils because of their sex, race, disability, religion or belief, or sexual orientation' (Department for Education, 2014a).

In addition, the UNESCO–IFLA School Libraries' Manifesto asserts: 'School library services must be provided equally to all members of the school community, regardless of age, race, gender, religion, nationality, language, professional or social status' (Oberg and Schultz-Jones, 2015). Clearly this is a statement about parity of access but we would like to take this one step further and declare that when identifying and understanding one's community for the purpose of teaching and learning we must do so by actively addressing differences. How do we ensure we reflect this in our library service to the school community? Our profession (like so many) is very white and mono-ethnic; if this is all that people see when they walk through the door then they may not implicitly identify with what we have to offer.

Margaret felt that her library was underused by the black students in the school and wondered why. She decided to ask some of the Year 9 students during their library lesson why they did not come to the library at other times of the day. She was surprised to hear that they did not feel comfortable in the space as there were no black students working in the library. She decided to invite a more diverse range of students to become library helpers and to promote the service throughout the school. She was delighted at the response and enthusiasm she received. By the end of term she saw a more representative cultural mix of students working and relaxing in the library.

Margaret found a way to increase diversity in the school library where she worked, but in practice can we meet the needs of everyone within the community? There are many competing demands and often as solo practitioners it is necessary to choose where to focus our energies in order to achieve maximum effect.

Sometimes our view of priorities is not the same as those of others in the school and it is common for the interests of different groups to clash. Any individual may have different needs at different times and these may shift rapidly in the course of a library visit. The need for a quiet work environment demonstrates this perfectly. For example, when sixth formers (aged 16–18) have a deadline to meet they want to be left in peace to get on with their work, but as soon as each one of them finishes they may want to use the library as a social space, regardless of their peers who are still working. It is no small challenge to balance all of these sorts of demands.

John, the learning resource centre manager at a large co-educational comprehensive, ran an extensive library programme, frequently holding lessons in the resource centre, which was popular and well used. However, each year in the early summer term parts of the area were used for oral language exams and silent sixth form study. John observed that neither group of users were using the resources, merely taking up space and preventing access to those in need of books and other resources. John found himself making up boxes to be sent to classrooms while trying to maintain silence in the working area. He pointed out the impasse to his line manager and showed him a list of classes that had requested access to the library. As a result the oral exams were relocated and an empty classroom was provided for silent sixth form study the following year.

It can be very difficult when we are striving to put our service at the heart of teaching and learning to find that the library is more highly valued as a nice space for meetings than as a facility for students. We need to ensure that our judgement is not clouded by parochial and territorial feelings but is rooted in what is for the good of our community. Appreciating pressures on such things as space is part of understanding our school and we will discuss our responses to these demands in the next chapter.

Defining our community will lead us to consider the many special groups within it, each with their particular requirements. It is impossible to provide an exhaustive list of possibilities, but some are suggested in Table 4.1.

Of course, each school is different and that is why we need to explore our own community through research.

What informs the ways we explore our community?

There are many ways to identify and come to understand one's community and the processes we select initially may well reveal which discourse of professionalism is our greatest influence at that time. These discourses are described in Chapter 1.

A technical-rational or managerial approach might involve studying

Table 4.1 Members of the school library community	
Type of library user	**Requirements and points to consider**
More able students	Virtual and physical collaborative space Communication via new technology Broadening horizons, e.g. displays Wider reading, e.g. booklists to prepare for university interviews Cultural events and activities
Students with specific learning difficulties	Guided reading scheme Paired-reading club Audio and visual facilities Mobile learning technologies Communication via new technology Homework assistance Tactile and kinesthetic materials Physical access Intellectual access
Students for whom English is an additional language	Online and print Graded reading scheme Foreign language dictionaries Mother tongue materials Visual dictionaries Audio and visual facilities
Keen readers or reluctant readers	Wide range of material in differing formats and media Reading clubs Virtual and physical collaborative space Communication via new technology
Older students or younger students	Zoning Wide range of material in differing formats and media Appropriate furniture and furnishings Age-appropriate displays Remote access to library resources
Classes of students	Class activities and group work Virtual and physical collaborative space Communication via new technology
Leisure users	Mobile learning technologies Activities, games and puzzles Music
Teaching staff and support staff	Staff loans Professional development collections Enquiry service Homework help for children of staff Support and advice for use of learning technologies
Parents	Activities and events Loans Enquiry service Support and advice for use of learning technologies

our community through the use of resources. We might make observations during a specific time period, use a questionnaire or gather statistical information from an automated cataloguing system. Reports from these systems can be complex and subdivided in various ways, for example by time periods, type of resource or resource media, year group, tutor group or class, or gender.

This data will enable patterns of borrowing to be discerned. Quantitative methods provide patterns of use but do not necessarily reveal reasons for those behavioural patterns. For instance, counting numbers of books borrowed might identify a class that borrows fewer books than others but it does not reveal whether the students who are borrowing books and other materials are reading them, enjoying them or developing their skills. Neither would the figures alone show whether the class borrowing fewer books is selecting more challenging material. Similarly these sorts of considerations would apply when counting hits on a website or database. One would have to make a further study, possibly involving carefully designed questionnaires and interview schedules, to build an understanding of the true patterns of library use (Gilham, 2005; Cohen, Manion and Morrison, 2007).

Taking a social democratic approach, we could begin with observation and discussion to identify the approaches to learning that are prevalent in the school. We might then use assessment for learning strategies (using assessment to support rather than to judge learning) to collect more information. If students use a feedback mechanism, such as a reading log, blog or online reviews linked to the resources used, they can assess their progress and in turn receive formative assessment from us. We will then have a much fuller picture of their engagement with reading in a range of formats.

The research approach that we adopt will be influenced by how the school sees the library and by the type of information it requires and deems relevant. In turn, a school's attitude to and use of its library will echo the prevalent theories of learning put into practice in the school (Todd, 2012; Kachel, 2013; Williams, Wavell and Morrison, 2013).

Ways of thinking about your learning community

When joining any organization it is important to study its mission statement, published policies, and development and improvement plans, including any online profile and social media presence. This enables us to understand how the organization presents itself and its priorities to the outside world. We should adopt a similar approach in our schools, and study the last inspection report and the school evaluation form. We need to identify the strategic view of the organization in order to be effective managers; this approach is examined in more detail in Chapter 5. If we accept that the core activities of schools are teaching and learning and that school librarians fulfil a crucial role in supporting these activities, then each individual librarian must find ways to promote teaching and learning in the school in which they work.

The school's own methods of evaluating itself will provide an understanding of where it considers its strengths and weaknesses to be. Identifying a weakness and developing work to contribute to addressing it is a beginning; how the school goes about this will demonstrate what type of learning community it is. Hargreaves (2000) helps us to think about the culture of our school so that we can understand our successes and failures within it. He writes of three cultures, which he labels as fragmented individualism, balkanization and contrived collegiality:

- In a school exhibiting fragmented individualism everyone operates as individuals with little discussion taking place between colleagues about teaching and learning.

- In a school with a balkanized culture colleagues form allegiances to small groups but little communication and co-operation takes place as a whole school.
- A school where collaboration is imposed by management will have contrived collegiality, with the mechanisms for its workings dictated rather than negotiated.

Several times in this book we have written about the isolation felt by some school librarians but Hargreaves helps us to understand that there are schools where some teachers also feel that they are working on their own. Appreciating what kind of school culture we find ourselves in will perhaps help us to see where we fit in and where difficulties we thought were ours alone might actually be shared. We might find that collaboration is still just an aspiration for teachers.

Wenger's theories (1998) about communities of practice and how we learn from each other are also relevant to our considerations. Does the school give regular time at meetings to share teaching practices? Are training days organized by the senior leadership team in consultation with staff? Wenger defines three characteristics for coherence of learning in a community:

- the engagement that defines the communities that we feel that we belong to
- negotiation of a joint enterprise, leading to building of mutual understandings
- a shared repertoire, which reflects activities from the mutual engagement.

In the space we have here we cannot do justice to the complexity and subtleties of Wenger's theoretical work but it is useful to consider the balance that needs to be achieved between participation and reification.

In the school library context, we participate with teachers to devise learning experiences for students jointly, review their success, and agree conclusions and ways forward. Reification is where such participation is made tangible by inclusion in a subject department's scheme of work.

Reification alone does not ensure a continuing role in teaching and learning for us. It is the participation in those relationships with teachers and students that is crucial. These relationships are much less tangible than many other library activities and so much harder to measure, but without them the library will not be seen as essential to raising literacy and attainment levels.

What does learning look like in our institutions?

Within any school there are a number of different approaches to learning adopted by different departments or even by individual teachers within a department. However, there is usually a dominant approach that is obvious in the school's paperwork and the way it communicates with the outside world about teaching and learning and student progress and behaviour.

If we really want to understand our school community we have to look beyond the library to find out how teaching and learning are viewed by our teachers and ourselves.

How are teachers in different departments in our schools supporting and encouraging learning and what are the implications for the library? Do we work differently with different departments?

School librarian Kathy organized an action research project with an A-level psychology group (17-year-old students). She and the teacher kept a log of what they saw during the lessons, using an online collaborative tool. Later they discussed their observations. This process enabled Kathy to see each lesson from the perspective of the teacher who was focused on the students' different levels of engagement and their progress in understanding. Kathy immediately realized that her observations were focused on the resources and how they were being used. For her part the teacher commented that Kathy's focus on skills made her realize that she needed to spend some lesson time developing these skills. At the end of the project Kathy concluded that to be effective in supporting teaching and learning she needed to identify students' current levels of understanding and work with them to move forward from where they were. Before her next lesson with the group she studied the students' essays with the teacher, to see how well the students had answered the essay question and what sort of support they needed in order to improve.

The resource focus that Kathy adopted in her observations was driven by her sense of responsibility for the resources. She was concerned about whether there were enough resources, whether they were at the right level for the students and how the students used them. Should she instead be focusing on the students and whether their understanding was being developed? This experience helped Kathy to develop her awareness of other aspects of learning and of how she might adapt her teaching to work more effectively. She found herself moving away from her behavioural approach towards the teacher's more constructivist perspective. Instead of transmitting information on how to go about researching a topic and assuming that this was sufficient, she now works closely with the teacher to identify students' weaknesses and focuses her teaching strategies to support their learning priorities. This project provided a powerful learning experience for both Kathy and the teacher she was working with. How can we engage in such effective learning within our schools? Is our school a true 'learning community'?

School librarian Nazir made a presentation to teaching staff about ways to deal with the 'cut and paste culture' among students. He made the link between homework tasks that fell into the first three levels of Bloom's Taxonomy of Educational Objectives (1956) as ones that lent themselves to cut and paste responses. Then he gave examples of tasks that involved the use of judgement and decision making, which linked to the higher-order thinking skills. Instead of setting students the task 'Find out about Martin Luther King' he asked them 'Compare Martin Luther King with Malcolm X and say who made the greater achievement to the civil rights movement'. Nazir's presentation was well received and a number of staff wanted to discuss ways of using the library for homework with him.

As a result of the sound pedagogic relationships that he had developed with teaching colleagues, Nazir had already discussed with them the problems of dealing with student focus on searching for and finding information online, at the expense of reading, evaluating and transforming the information in order to produce work. Using Bloom to illustrate his points and providing practical solutions to change the homework tasks from passive to active tasks, Nazir successfully identified the library with teaching and learning. By highlighting that he wanted to improve students' analytical skills and underlining the benefits to all of changing, Nazir succeeded in demonstrating his understanding of teaching priorities.

In order to develop a deeper understanding of approaches to teaching and learning in our school, it may be useful to consider one simple approach to categorizing learning as a quick overview. Table 4.2 on the next page gives a quick identification guide to approaches to teaching and learning in schools drawing on Webb (2013) and Kuhlthau (1993). This should help to identify some implications for how we teach information literacy in school libraries. It will help us match the information literacy offer to what approach we take to teaching and learning in our community, though no single approach is prevalent.

Table 4.2 Approaches to teaching and learning in schools

Style	Behavioural	Humanistic	Cognitive or constructive
Characteristics	• Instruction and delivery of factual information to students	• Concern for whole person: self-esteem, emotions, existing knowledge and skills • Involves learners in the delivery in a facilitative and co-operative style	• Individual or group learning through active learning by participants
Role of staff	• Organizer • Lecturer • Instructor	• Tutor • Adviser • Facilitator	• Counsellor or guide • Designer of learning tasks and problem-solving ideas
Teaching style	• Heavy structure sequencing small chunks of information with quick feedback • Didactic	• Facilitator • Students can ask for help • Opens a dialogue but teacher is leader	• Facilitator • Students are supported in their independent learning as needed • Student-driven learning
How information literacy fits in	• Instruction is linear	• Embedded across the curriculum information literacy model and delivered at the point of need	• Within student-centred support of independent learning

Most of us will have a favoured approach to teaching and learning as well as a preferred teaching style that suits us best and when asked to step outside that mode we will experience some discomfort. To be effective, we have to adapt to whichever role best suits the incoming teacher, class and purpose of the lesson. In considering preferred styles of working we may be able to see why we find it easier to collaborate with some teachers than others. Does our preferred style of working resonate with the prevalent approach to teaching and learning in our school? Current practice advocates a child-centred approach with teachers adapting to the individual learning needs of their students. Does this mean that information literacy should always be taught at the point of need and be related to personalized learning?

When school staff adopt a predominantly behavioural approach to teaching and learning they will tend to view the library as a store of resources that students may draw on to find facts for their assignments. When school staff adopt constructivist principles of learning they will integrate the library into enquiry-based activities designed to enhance students' thinking skills. If school staff adopt a humanist approach they will involve the library when and how students want to use it or when they want to engage them in learning in a different type of environment. This mix of approaches to teaching and learning may exist even between departments, individual teachers and philosophies of subject engagement with information. These generalizations of style may help us but we must always remember that in each school various approaches operate at the same time, sending out conflicting messages to students about learning and the role of the library in learning. The picture presented here is a simplified model of teaching and learning and does not reflect the full complexity of learning styles in practice.

What does learning look like for the individuals in our communities?

Theoretical thinking in different fields can provide illumination when we are working to identify and understand our community. For instance Maslow's theory of motivation and human behaviour (1998), although originally set out in 1954, remains relevant today and encapsulates some clear messages for us. One way of thinking about the role of the library is to adapt Maslow's hierarchy of needs to thinking about levels of service that the library can offer (Figure 4.1 on the next page).

Maslow believed that to progress from the base to the top of the pyramid achieved a lasting sense of satisfaction. Since meeting basic

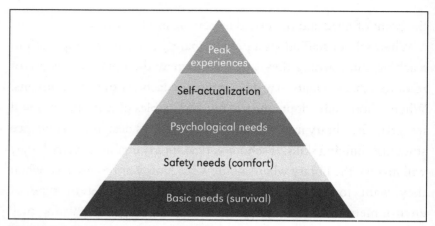

Figure 4.1 Maslow's hierarchy of needs

needs is fundamental to survival, we might think of the library in a physical sense as a place of shelter. A teacher or student might interpret this less dramatically as a requirement to provide a service, for example responding to users' urgent information needs with understanding and speed. The second stage could be thought of as the need to provide nice seating, but perhaps users might think that clear boundaries and a feeling of being welcomed are more crucial to comfort levels. We know from our experience that we like to be acknowledged; to feel included is very important for our happiness in the workplace. Teachers and students have the same psychological needs; we all struggle with a sense of isolation at times. As we discussed earlier, we should be aware of the diversity in our community and ensure all feel welcome in our library. If we want people to be good learners, they need the confidence to take risks. We believe that the library plays a key role in enabling students to develop the self-esteem fundamental to risk taking (Devonshire et al., 2014). 'Peak experiences' are the points at which people grow and experience fulfilment. For learners these might be those 'light bulb moments' that sometimes occur where a concept suddenly makes sense; sometimes a teacher recognizes that this has happened at the same time.

We should also be mindful of our online communities. Has the digital environment changed the way people learn and where it takes place? In the past we could rely on a stable pattern of people walking through the library doors to use resources. Now the emphasis is moving from the library to the librarian. How does the librarian facilitate learning with those who never enter the library?

School librarian Eve attended a school training day led by a university lecturer in teaching and learning. He invited the group to discuss what services teenagers would expect from a modern library and librarian. Together the delegates painted a picture of a group with high expectations of online and digital resources who are strategic learners and prefer to find out by experimentation and collaboration with friends rather than asking for help. This made Eve rethink a talk that she gives every year to all Year 11 (15–16 year olds) classes as they embark on a piece of discursive writing for English. Previously she had sat them at the tables and shown them useful paper resources. She did mention some websites but felt that it was more important to show them the books, believing the students would never discover them for themselves. This time Eve took advantage of the school's bring your own device policy and allowed them to use their personal laptops, tablets and phones in the library. She gave them suggestions for a variety of sources they might use in both digital and print form and then asked them to feed back to the group which resources they had found most useful and which they would like to share with others. Eve found that the students valued resources in all forms for different reasons and for their usefulness for different aspects of the task set. She also noticed that the students felt more comfortable with their mobile devices to hand. Teacher feedback suggested that the quality of work produced was better than it had been in the past.

A Demos report (Birdwell and Bani, 2014) has identified a subset of the 'Millennials' as Generation Citizen (Millennials – students born between 1997 and 2000). Tara Walpert Levy, Managing Director of Google, suggests that this generation 'thrive on connection, community, creation and curation; they're engaged and they want their voices to be heard' (Levy, 2013). Recognition of these attributes has led to an increase in innovative approaches to teaching and learning such as the 'flipped classroom'; this reverses traditional teaching by engaging students with content before the class, often online (such as viewing a short video lecture at home), which is then followed up in class using exercises, projects, discussions, etc. to check on and extend student understanding. (For more about this see Bishop, 2013.) This is an interesting example of how the digital environment can change the structure of learning.

The experience of being a learner can help us gain unexpected insights into service improvement. Engaging in a process of analysing learners' experience coupled with understanding how to manage any resulting change and innovation in their behaviour (see Chapter 9) should be our *raison d'etre*.

The growing acceptance of allowing students to use their devices in schools has led to a cultural change even in the digital world; as we have seen in the vignette about Eve above, this has advantages in that every classroom and library can now function as a flexible IT space and in other ways. This enables all the resources in libraries to be used within the same environment. However, increased use of social media had also rendered teenagers even more image conscious than in the past because of the speed at which issues such as cyber-bullying can develop. They may think that the library is not 'cool' and not wish to be seen using it by their peers. In addition there is a time factor in visiting the library for any library user and advances in technology such as websites, digital books and online journals have lessened the need for a physical presence. Librarians now have to consider how we will reach out to our community and create libraries without walls if we are to deliver our service and expertise effectively.

A virtual library can enhance the presence of the library service and resources in the wider community and in particular strengthen home–school links. Social media is an excellent forum to promote a brand or image for the library allowing collaboration, discussion and feedback from various sectors of the community.

An understanding of how our community operates and its cultural ethos requires us to move from superficial concerns to gain a real insight into how the community works and learns in order to grasp how libraries can best serve it. Inevitably this throws up conflicts and dichotomies. However, our community is dynamic and so as librarians we have to be prepared to change as our users' needs do by engaging in three key processes: analysing learners and types of learning within the community, consequently innovating to meet these needs, and managing the necessary changes. This cyclical process repeats endlessly so we can ensure that our service to the community is appropriate and as up to date as possible. The next chapter will look at ways to respond when clashes arise.

CHAPTER 5

Making a positive response to challenges

Getting into position

Developing relationships requires energy and that needs to come from us. It takes time to build trust and confidence between people, especially in such a hectic work environment as a school, so persistence and resilience is essential. How can librarians stay positive when, as we have seen, others are unlikely to find the time or energy to come to us with ideas? We need to ensure that we position ourselves so that we can capitalize on possible opportunities and this depends on us being alert, proactive and determined. Our aim should be that in the longer term, when our role is well established in the minds of senior leadership and staff, we will automatically be involved in the school decision-making process.

Good positioning requires research and awareness on our part. Who are the budget holders in the school? What are the current big projects (e.g. demonstrating pupil progress, social inclusion for all, independent learning)? When we have answered these questions we should consider how and what we can contribute. If we can go to a project manager with a proposal or solution this will allow us to be identified as someone who is knowledgeable, who participates and can be relied on.

In the first instance, we are our own best resource. We have expertise and skills. We should market our wares with shrewdness.

What is possible in the real world of school libraries?

Three major issues faced by most school librarians are accommodation, budget and staffing. How can we respond positively to these challenges?

Accommodation

Few schools have all the space they need and not all school libraries are able to accommodate one-tenth of the school's population at any one time, as recommended by Barrett and Douglas (2004), or even one class, as recommended by CILIP (Shaper, 2014). Does this prevent us from making an impact on teaching and learning? Lack of space can be extremely frustrating, yet many librarians fulfil a vital role in spite of this difficulty. The following vignettes show two responses to lack of space.

In a school of 1500, there were seats for only 45 students in the library. In the lobby at the entrance to the library there was a group of ancient filing cabinets containing a range of resources, including newspaper clippings and other items now available online. Lynda, the school librarian, surveyed the teaching staff asking them to rank in importance what they would like to use the library for. One highly rated recommendation was for there to be room for group work. As a result the filing cabinets were removed and the space was used to create an area for small group work.

Lynda succeeded in making the staff feel that their teaching priorities were of first consideration in the library. In the next vignette, teaching and learning are the key drivers in the librarian's decision-making process.

Staff in the Science Department wanted to book their Year 8 (12 year olds) classes into the library to use resources about renewable energy. Timetable and library space constraints meant that it was not possible to accommodate everyone. So the librarian, Deesha, created a book box for the classes that could not be fitted in and made materials available on the virtual learning environment. The resources could be moved to wherever the learning was taking place in the science laboratories and at home. Deesha supported the Science Department's teaching effectively. Although not all the classes were able to use the library space directly, a compromise was achieved that benefited all.

One way to approach library development in a situation fraught with constraints is to make an analysis of strengths, weakness, opportunities and threats (SWOT). This enables the librarian to focus on the strengths, weaknesses, opportunities and threats that affect the library. The most effective way of doing this is to involve the teachers and students, but we can begin the process on our own (see Appendix 4). This problem-solving approach, particularly when seen through the eyes of others, can lead the librarian to identify new openings and enables us to choose our priorities informed by our community's opinions.

We believe that it is important to be seen to provide a service, not only physically through the supply of resources, but also intellectually by having a profile in the school as someone who is knowledgeable about educational as well as library issues. This should be our area of expertise when working in a school library, in the same way as if we were working in a library specializing in agriculture, when we would have to be aware of both agricultural information sources and the current issues affecting the sector to be effective when dealing with enquiries.

We can establish ourselves in the eyes of teaching colleagues by using informal conversations with them to show ourselves to be equally committed to students' education and potential collaborators. This is the process of group development referred to in Chapter 1, particularly the 'storming' and 'norming' stages (Forsyth, 2006).

Budget

Even though few librarians have generous budgets that cover everything that they could possibly want to purchase, they are still able to make a positive response to the challenge of having a limited budget. Some librarians are extremely clever at finding ways to supplement their buying power, negotiating with subject leaders to share costs of purchases, making bids for external grants, lobbying the parent–teacher association and, most importantly, identifying key budgets in the school, demonstrating to the holder how the library can contribute to that area and requesting to be included in the budget plan.

Establishing a track record with budget holders by providing them with an evidence base is a useful strategy in attracting continuing funding, as Mercy demonstrates in this vignette.

The library in Mercy's school is one of the first places that the head teacher and senior leadership team consider when allocating resources. One of the main reasons for this is that Mercy is always able to demonstrate a clear audit trail between expenditure and its impact on student learning. Projects are always evaluated and reports given to budget holders. Results are expressed in numbers and by assessing individual student learning. Nothing speaks more powerfully to the head teacher than the students' own voices:

'It has made me read some authors that I would never have thought about reading' (John).

So, is there a point at which a lack of funding makes it impossible for a librarian to make a positive response to the challenge of having limited resources? The answer to this question is related to a number of other factors. There are many librarians who are engaged in supporting pupil progress despite having limited resources. They have managed to secure an active role within the curriculum through using what is available creatively and by looking beyond resourcing issues to other contributions they can make, such as sharing professional knowledge to support the extended project qualification offered by some UK schools. Only individuals can decide whether they can respond positively to a lack of funding; clearly there are many librarians with only small budgets and few computers who still manage to foster a love of reading and enquiry.

Staffing

The other major resource that many librarians lack is clerical support. This is needed to maintain adequate opening hours, and to maintain supervision throughout the school day, enabling the librarian to carry out their professional activities effectively. In the absence of an assistant, the librarian needs to make choices about levels of service provision. Should the running of the issue desk be prioritized over developmental work? Should volunteers be organized to help (in itself a potentially time-consuming job for the librarian), or should the library be closed to everyone else while the librarian is engaged with a class or club activity? Is access to the library at all times, regardless of whether or not it is supervised, the most important consideration? Librarians have varying viewpoints because our priorities are based on our individual professional values and the nature of the community in which we work. Ultimately, choice of service level is determined by our head teacher and the senior leadership team, but their decisions need to be fully informed. We need to ask ourselves if our senior leadership team is aware of the possible alternatives to questions of staffing and their implications.

Dale was very upset when told that the library assistant in the school library would be required to work part-time on the school's main reception desk. She thought very carefully about how she could make the point that the cuts could have a serious impact on services while being wary of proposing something which she was not prepared to live with. She produced a short and factual report as a basis for discussions with her line manager outlining the following possible options:

- closing the library to students and staff at break time each day
- maintaining only two of the four 'reading challenges'
- cutting back before-school opening hours from 8 a.m. to 8.30 a.m.

She then wrote about the impact that these would have on her library targets and the school's priorities for inclusion and for promoting reading for pleasure across the curriculum. Her intention was to point out to the head teacher the implications of reducing the staffing hours of the library assistant in the library. By clearly identifying links between staffing levels and learning outcomes and without even voicing disagreement with the proposal to change the library assistant's working arrangements, Dale subtly outlined the impact of the proposed reduction in library staffing levels.

By speaking the language of the line manager and taking a clear minded, strategic, management approach to this resourcing problem,

Dale made it possible to achieve an acceptable solution. She made visible the link between her work and the students' learning and attainment, which is the school's main priority.

Making a difference

Are we saying that size, money and staffing do not matter? Of course not. These things do matter a very great deal, but the most significant resource of all is ourselves. It is possible to make a difference while experiencing a weakness in one or all of these areas. Every school has challenges. Whether we are able to make a positive response to them and sustain it depends on our individual context and what it offers us. One librarian may feel that without adequate resources he cannot contribute. Another may decide that as long as she is involved in the school's decision-making processes and is seen as a colleague she can move forward. Each of us needs to ask ourselves how much has to be in place for us to make a positive response.

Senior leaders have the ultimate responsibility for deciding what level and type of facilities they provide for students and staff. However, we can influence these choices by explaining what difference the decisions senior leaders make will have on the service offered in the library. In presenting evidence and analysis we are fulfilling our role. We are doing the best that we can for the library and its users. Ways of generating and using evidence about the service we provide are discussed in Chapter 6.

Tapping in to school priorities

As already noted, the world of education is increasingly driven by targets and government initiatives and in the UK these are reflected in schools' planning and self-evaluation procedures. Tuning in to these priorities is vital. How can we demonstrate that the library is helping the school to meet its targets? By reflecting the school's priorities in the library's planning and evaluations we can contribute to whole school objectives. In Chapter 7 we discuss how analysing library activities is useful in building the whole picture of how a school meets its targets.

One way for school librarians to contribute to the school's priorities is to take on new roles, such as literacy or careers co-ordinators, exam invigilators or cover supervisors. Some of these roles complement the librarian's role and enable us to provide a useful extension of it; others may be taken on because there is little choice. Are we taking on roles out of a desperation to be included and seen as valuable? What impact might these new roles have on our librarian role, for its benefit or to its detriment?

Angela was a Chartered librarian with a master's degree in education who enjoyed her work in a large secondary school library. However, she sometimes got bored and frustrated because her colleagues did not use the library with their classes as much as she wished they would. In order to make herself more visible around the school Angela got involved in helping with the costumes for the school play. This helped her build relationships with students beyond the library. Like many librarians, she was a good organizer so she then offered to sort out the arrangements for taking school photographs. Her efficiency was noted and soon she was asked to manage other administrative tasks, which made her realize that this might not be what she wanted to become known for. So, when she was approached to become a form tutor she had to think hard about the impact this would have on her position. It was a qualitatively different role from the administrative jobs she had previously undertaken and it could raise her status in the eyes of the students.

In order to decide whether to become a form tutor Angela has to weigh up carefully the issues of time management and her profile and status within the school. Would becoming a form tutor raise her status in the eyes of students? Would it give her new opportunities to interact? What would be the impact on the library services? Would form tutor duties take her away from her primary role in the library?

Unfortunately, librarians are not always part of the forward planning process in a school and may not be kept informed about it as a matter of course. The danger then is that the library's planning and evaluations take place in isolation and are not seen as supporting the organization's shared vision. We must have ways of finding out what is going on. Attending school meetings is essential so that we can understand what proposals will affect students and teachers. Networking with other librarians and reading the professional literature is sometimes the first source of information about a new initiative. Contributing such information in our workplace enriches the decision making of the school and demonstrates that we have wide expertise and experience.

If the library's improvement plan is devised in isolation, the librarian may well be putting forward a vision that nobody else understands or will support. By using the framework established for all middle leaders in a school, reviewing and setting development targets, we identify ourselves to others as a member of that team. Do our development objectives form a personal wish list or are they rooted in school priorities? Is the theme or issue considered a priority for the school? We need to find out what conditions an initiative needs for development and understand how it will contribute to teaching and learning. We also need to ensure that our targets are SMART: 'specific, measurable, achievable, relevant and time-bound' (Invensis, 2011) or 'specific, measurable, agreed, realistic and timed' (BBC, 2014).

How do we make line-management systems work for us?

We need to build up contacts within school and the obvious person to begin with is our line manager. There is a mixed pattern of line management for school libraries in the UK with this responsibility being undertaken by head teachers, deputy head teachers, heads of subject departments, teachers, bursars, media resources officers, network managers or administration officers. Line management clearly affects the positioning of the library in the organization. For example, if the library's line manager is at the heart of curriculum development, then logically the library will be drawn in as a tool for those activities. If the line manager is remote from academic decision making then this may well result in the library being isolated from major school developments.

Again, in the UK, ultimately our actions feed into formal performance review and this should be a process where the line manager develops a sense of all that we do, regardless of their specialism. At its best, the performance management procedure will offer the librarian a much-needed opportunity to brainstorm problems, find out what is going on in the school and be challenged or inspired by that line manager.

If the librarian is line managed by a support staff member such as the media resources officer or the finance manager this may mean that the librarian's role is identified as supporting resourcing but not actively identified with supporting teaching and learning. This may be agreeable to both school and librarian. Where school librarians see the library's role as central to teaching and learning, as in the social democratic model outlined in Chapter 1, they may find it difficult to make progress in such work with a line manager who is a member of the support staff.

Caroline had been in post as a school librarian at her school for several years and was line managed by the finance manager. Caroline found it difficult to be involved in the academic life of the school because her line manager blocked any moves that she deemed to be sidestepping her authority. Consequently Caroline did not attend curriculum meetings, which led to her being unaware of the introduction of new courses. She tried to access information by sitting with teachers at coffee breaks but this caused a rift with the office staff, who felt snubbed. Caroline also felt that she was poorly served by the line-management process because the finance manager did not have the academic insight to be able to guide and challenge her.

Caroline had to decide whether to make the best of the situation or seek a new position elsewhere. Line managers can be good and bad; each has their strengths and weaknesses. The head teacher's view of the library is critical to its inclusion in the life of the school but does that make him or her a good line manager for the library? As the following vignette shows, it is beneficial if the line manager is senior, part of the academic staff, but essentially supports the library's role.

Natalie had been line managed by the head teacher but he had little time to meet her and develop the work of the library. So, it was proposed that the line management of the library should be circulated among the deputy head teachers yearly. Initially, Natalie was very disappointed because the first deputy head to take over the task, although very supportive in their meetings, often failed to follow through on agreed actions. The next deputy head, however, was very clear about her vision of how the library should contribute to the life of a school and supported Natalie's work vigorously at senior leadership level.

Relationships between librarian and line manager need at least to be functional for successful work to take place. In reality, personality always plays a part. A line manager may be well placed to further the role of the library but it should be acknowledged that if the chemistry between those involved is tainted in some way that will affect the success of the relationship.

A hostile line manager can make it impossible for the librarian to progress; however, if a line manager is merely apathetic then it is still feasible to find ways forward. It might be that line management could be considered a matter for administration purposes only. To use a little business jargon, if our activities are part of the deliverables in someone else's area of responsibility other than the library line manager, then it is logical to report those matters directly to that person. After all, if an English teacher wished to undertake a cross-curricular piece of work involving science, he or she would talk to a science colleague. They would not consider being line managed by the head of English as a barrier to working with someone in another department. A pragmatic approach requires us to make judgements about what makes things work and then to pursue those actions.

How we conduct our business and interact with others sets a value in the eyes of students and members of staff. All who work in a school contribute to its overall aim – education. If everyone drives in the same direction, understanding the value of their role and how it contributes, the organization is much more likely to achieve its goals. We believe that to lose sight of that is the pathway to marginalization for a librarian.

How do we use other relationships to help us?

It is important to understand how we are seen and many potential perceptions of school librarians have been examined in Chapter 2. We must make a positive response:

- as a leader
- as a manager
- by making the most of the line management available to us
- by building good relationships.

Identifying people's areas of responsibility, showing an interest, finding ways to contribute and volunteering for working parties are all ways to exercise influence and foster relationships. We can build on all these opportunities to realize our vision of the library's role. It is essential for those who operate within the social democratic model, as discussed in Chapter 1, to pursue these options for success. Figures of influence are not necessarily senior post-holders; the way someone operates may give them influence over others.

Timing is important. If an external inspection report highlights a need, such as to stretch the most able, the librarian can seize the opportunity and focus energy. This might happen as a conversation with staff to gauge feeling and understanding before deciding how to contribute. Would it be helpful to find the latest material on this topic and supply key people with copies? Doing so would certainly show that the librarian has their finger on the pulse.

A small health warning at this point might be wise – we should choose our projects carefully. Too many tasks may lead to feeling overburdened and possibly unable to manage with all the work that they entail. Action requires us to take initiative and this may take several forms:

- wait and be told (lowest initiative)
- ask what to do
- recommend, then take resulting action
- act, but advise at once
- act alone, then routinely report (highest initiative)

(Oncken and Wass, 1999).

Oncken and Wass (1999) cleverly identify the behaviours of the wise manager and those of the conventional subordinate. Where would we classify our behaviour in relation to other middle and senior leaders in the school? We need to beware of too many burdens being placed on our shoulders that rightly should sit elsewhere. As Oncken and Wass make clear, good time management involves more than the ability to prioritize tasks, it is essentially a matter of identifying the most relevant management behaviour to achieve a necessary goal.

School priorities can be identified and tackled through the established planning and review processes. Decisions and choices about where the library should focus need to be based on evidence derived from any of a variety of evaluation methods. This evidence can also be used to demonstrate the library's contribution to school objectives or to secure support for library needs. We can advance our vision of the library's role by engaging in these processes and crucially by building relationships with others. Collaboration with others and the power of pedagogic partnerships will be covered in Chapter 7.

Learning from students

In making a positive response, good managers take the initiative and use the appropriate tools to evaluate, analyse and make decisions. Our relationships with teachers provide an excellent conduit to enable the library to work with students, but we also have direct experiences of working with students every day. How can we tune in to the priorities of these users?

Openness to ideas is a useful quality in a librarian and will be discussed in Chapter 7. Ideas can spring from all directions. We are always hearing from our students, but actively listening to their suggestions and reasons for their proposals can sometimes be eye-opening. Eliciting the student voice has become popular. Often this takes the form of establishing a student council in the school whose focus is frequently on matters to do with the learning environment. The original principle behind capturing and distilling the student voice is to involve students in decisions about the learning process and develop their skills as student researchers (Fielding and Bragg 2003; Rogers and Frost, 2006).

What are the priorities for our students when using the library? Do they want a warm, safe place, access to a computer and someone at hand to help with their homework? Near the end of a lesson in the library we could ask a few students to tell us what has helped them the most and if there is something that could be improved to make it a better lesson next time. In itself this is a source of learning for us and it may well help form some evidence useful in demonstrating the link between the library and learning. Another approach, in the spirit of understanding students as researchers, could involve asking students to interview each other briefly and then report back. Assessment for learning can work both ways.

As we have discussed, what is written in a school or library improvement plan is not necessarily what the teachers are actually worrying about. What is stated in a policy does not always reflect actual practice. When a librarian sees an opportunity, it might not come to fruition if colleagues have different ideas. As librarians, we face these ups and downs every day of our working lives and we have to choose where to place our energies to achieve maximum benefit.

How well are we doing?

Our individual vision and personal standards determine the answer to this question. When confronted with an attractive but empty library, one person might take the view that the service is in place and if loan figures are low and class visits rare this is not the librarian's responsibility. Another would want to know why the library was not used and how things could be changed. Similarly, one librarian with a busy library would happily create graphs for the annual report showing high borrowing figures, while another practitioner would conduct research to show their impact on teaching and learning. In our opinion, this last image is at the very core of what makes a librarian working in the education sector effective.

There are many useful books that tell us the key principles of library management (e.g. Lemaire and Duncan, 2014; Shaper, 2014), but it is experience that develops leadership. Evaluation is more than filling in a form; it can provide a trigger for all that a professional does to enhance their perception and performance. Librarians can influence, lead the learning of others and contribute to change. To make the positive response that characterizes leadership, we must surface above our day-to-day concerns and draw on our excitement and passion, to bring inspiration, innovation and integration to our work.

CHAPTER 6

Generating and using evidence of impact

Evaluating what we do is a crucial part of our professional practice. We work as librarians in order to make a difference for others but how do we know if we are succeeding if we do not evaluate? How can we persuade others of the value of our work without having evidence to support our claims? For example, head teachers want to see a return on the investment made in the library and evaluation evidence helps to make its impact visible. Practice that is evidence-based has credibility in the eyes of others and enables us to demonstrate the library's strategic role and improve services. In addition, active use of evidence reflects the wider move across education towards evidence-based practice. We need to be seen working at that level.

It is important not only to generate our own evidence, but also to keep up to date and actively use published research to raise awareness of the possibilities that school librarians can offer and the conditions most likely to make any initiative effective. This chapter will look at using both published evidence and standards, and evidence we generate ourselves.

Using published evidence
Some useful examples of published evidence

There is now a good body of published evidence from which the school librarian can draw to inform a course of action they are considering, or to support a case they are trying to make.

One useful source is a critical review of the published evidence on the impact of school libraries (Williams, Wavell and Morrison, 2013), which brought together a range of studies from different countries. It is important that school librarians know about, and use, this type of material because of its credibility. Williams and her colleagues cited a well known series of large-scale statistical studies conducted in a number of American states and a Canadian province, from Colorado (Lance, Rodney and Hamilton-Pennell, 2000) to New York (Small et al., 2007), which found a direct correlation between a well staffed and resourced school library and higher test scores for all student grades (Scholastic Research Foundation, 2008). The quality and volume of this statistical evidence combined with other more qualitative case studies enable us to make claims about the value of school libraries that are well supported. The research by Williams, Wavell and Morrison (2013) also identified what we need to do and what needs to be in place, if we are to have an impact (summarized in Figure 6.1), providing us with credible evidence we can use both to develop our practice and to make a case for resources.

Other important and useful documents produced in the UK include the report of the School Libraries Commission (Morris, 2010), which contains a valuable picture of practice and a number of recommendations, including of changes that can be initiated by individual librarians. This report was partly based on evidence generated by a national survey of UK school libraries (Streatfield, Shaper and Rae-Scott, 2010), which led to several articles published for different audiences: teachers, governors and librarians (e.g. Shaper and Streatfield, 2012).

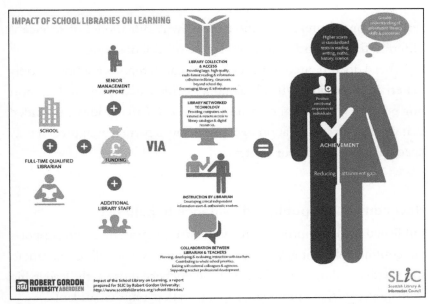

Figure 6.1 The impact of school libraries on learning when given adequate resources (Williams, Wavell and Morrison, 2013)

The report of the Libraries All Party Parliamentary Group (2014), based on a survey of head teachers, could have credibility in the eyes of current head teachers. The recommendations of a peer group are always influential.

Standards and guidelines for school libraries have been published by organizations around the world (IFLA, 2006; American Association of School Libraries, 2007; Valenza, 2010; California Department for Education, 2011; School Library Association, 2011; Shaper, 2014) and provide models for best practice against which we can evaluate our services and develop our practice. Comparison with models of this kind provides an opportunity for reflection and analysis to see how far our service meets these standards. However when using standards it is important to remember that these represent ideals, a vision of what could be, otherwise it is possible to feel overwhelmed by the inherent expectations. These inspirational texts do not always acknowledge the reality of our contexts and the reasons why our model of service is different from the one envisaged by the official documents.

Official documents and large-scale research reports are not the only materials to consider when looking for evidence to guide and support our practice. Individual case studies can offer many ideas, provided that we use our imagination to explore how a particular approach may need adapting to suit our context.

How can we use published evidence to help us?

Published evidence provides us with current awareness and supports our continued learning. We can then select items that will be relevant to share with our different audiences: head teachers, those in the leadership team, governors, teaching staff, support staff, parents or students.

Inside our schools we can use up-to-date research and advocacy materials as evidence when making a proposal to senior leadership, to help persuade them that the library needs these additional funds, or specific support to meet its target. Evidence about the impact on learning made by school libraries could help top and tail a proposal for a specific project, in order to inform and persuade the reader that the resourcing required by it will yield tangible results. We may also use published evidence internally to help transform people's viewpoints, to show them what other school libraries are doing and what can be achieved.

Across a group of schools, the Scottish review (Williams, Wavell and Morrison, 2013) or the School Library Commission report (Morris, 2010) could be used to persuade head teachers in a local area of the value that a good library can add to a school's outcomes. On a local level published material shared between colleagues contributes to our collective professional development. Sharing published evidence on outcomes and processes that help deliver good services, either informally through networking and social media or formally, in articles and at conferences is a valuable contribution to the wider profession.

At a national level librarians belonging to national organizations can harness published evidence in promotional material and on websites to design resources that can be used as evidence for advocacy. This can help librarians who may feel isolated in their schools while also demonstrating the importance and value of school libraries and librarians to a wider audience. For example the School Library Group of CILIP Scotland has developed an advocacy strategy. This highlights the positive contribution school libraries and librarians make in supporting the curricular and developmental needs of younger people as well as their impact on students' learning and well-being (CILIP in Scotland, 2014).

Generating and using our evidence

We will look at both evaluation and assessment to examine how we can generate evidence strategically to increase our effectiveness and provide evidence of our impact. Generating and using such evidence is part of a wider culture in education driven by the pressures to make learning visible. The terms evaluation and assessment are often used interchangeably and this can lead to confusion so we will define these at the outset. Evaluation sets out to study the value, effectiveness and experience of a service, programme or activity. Assessment refers to judging whether learning has taken place for an individual or group of learners. The outcomes of assessment provide an important source of data when designing an evaluation of the library service.

Any evaluation ideally requires data from more than one source so that evidence can be triangulated and a three-dimensional picture be created. For example, we may collect systematic feedback from students, reactions from relevant teachers, and observations of how students are using specific resources. Bringing these together will enable our evaluation to have greater reliability and credibility. In addition we need to approach evaluation with open minds, ready to capture the unexpected because our work with students and colleagues often has unintended, unpredicted effects. These may be positive or negative but it is these surprises that can make researching our practice so satisfying. Good evaluation allows us to examine the perceptions of others, to see matters through their eyes and reflect on what we find. Understanding the original purpose of the activity will help us focus the evaluation. What was the objective we wished to accomplish? What do we want students or teachers to do differently? Analysis of the evidence generated allows us to make interpretations, which can be communicated to others and provide a foundation for future decisions regarding the library service.

If you want to pursue this further we recommend two useful sources to help you manage an evaluation: Markless and Streatfield (2013) have written about the evaluation of impact, and *CILIP Guidelines for Secondary School Libraries* (Shaper, 2014) includes a section on the management of evaluation.

How can we make learning in the library visible to others?

Evaluation takes place at different levels: formally at senior leadership level, with governors and school inspections; semi-formally for internal management processes; and informally to cultivate better practices. We need to choose carefully what to evaluate in order to maximize the outcome of our efforts on behalf of the library service. The choice also needs to be manageable given the resources and time available to us. It would be politic to choose an aspect that resonates with government policy and is therefore a school priority. An example in UK schools would be a focus on reading for pleasure as this is currently part of inspection criteria. We may choose to evaluate a reading club. At the outset we must establish aims, objectives and a baseline by asking ourselves questions such as, what is the purpose of the reading club? Does it target specific groups of children? Does it aim to be inclusive of the school community? Who took part? What was the nature of their reading habit and experience before the activity? What effects are felt by those who take part? What is the nature of the difference it makes for them?

To answer these questions we need both quantitative and qualitative data:

Quantitative data: Are we reaching our target audience? Is the school community well represented among the participants? For instance we could analyse
— a baseline from established records for reading or use a short questionnaire at the outset;
— books borrowed, tried, completed, loved or hated using a reader's log sheet or evidence via discussions.
Qualitative data: Are there stories from a range of students which can show detailed impact on individuals?

The following vignette gives an example of how evidence might be captured.

School librarian Kathryn found it difficult to get good quality data from questionnaires on how the reading club affected the development of student reading. Students did not engage very deeply with this method. So Kathryn created an active session, using Post-it notes and a display board, where students were asked to comment on why they took part in the reading club and what difference it had made for them. Then she displayed the covers of the books they had read and asked the students to share their responses to the stories and stick the Post-it notes next to each one. The students really enjoyed giving their opinions, discussing them with each other as they moved about the space, writing on the Post-its and sticking them up. The students ended the session feeling their opinions were valued and Kathryn photographed the process and final displays as her evidence.

Once we have some data, the next step is to transform this evidence into a format tailored to the people we need to convince. We need to decide who would be most interested in reading this evaluation and what type of report is appropriate. For example, we might write:

- a report to the leadership team highlighting relevance to their target areas, e.g. targeting Pupil Premium students with details of individual progress
- an executive summary style report to the head teacher to secure additional funding
- a complete report for the school librarian's line manager to contribute evidence for our performance review.

Evaluation to retain visibility

We do not always have to undertake resource-heavy evaluations. We may wish to draw attention to something that is going well or to the wide range of work that we are doing. In that case we have a lower burden of proof. For example we can evaluate our reading club in a more informal way by putting three open questions online and using this as a basis for a short feedback to the senior leadership team.

A survey can be undertaken to solicit student voice to acquire data relevant to a particular topic, for example personal reading habits, use of electronic devices, value placed on different library activities, or knowledge of information literacy. Data of this kind can be used to feed into the decision-making processes of the library and relevant pieces could be presented to others in school for whom it may provide useful insights. For instance one might find out what percentage own a smart phone and what percentage use it for revision? This knowledge could highlight a need for future guidance that can easily be provided and would be valued by senior leaders if brought to their attention. It is useful to think about the possible range of audiences for whom the data may have relevance before making any evaluation.

We can share the outcomes of our work less formally, for example by:

- sending a letter to parents recognizing a child's participation, hard work and progress as a reader
- setting up a display in an area easily seen by the head teacher and leadership team
- writing a short report to the English Department, showing the links between the evaluation outcomes and the assessment criteria of the English curriculum, thereby demonstrating how the library contributes to their priorities
- writing a letter inviting an appropriate governor to participate in a library activity
- using a social media opportunity with a photo of student work in response to a particular author's book.

Does the library have an academic monitoring role?

As we mentioned earlier, assessment is an important source of data that can be used when evaluating a library activity. Should we get involved in assessment? In the eyes of the leadership team assessment evidence is highly significant. Can we use this to our advantage? Certainly one can contribute to the evidence collected by deputy head teachers for provision maps, which record work done with a target student group. The next vignette shows how a librarian got involved in academic monitoring.

White, Pupil Premium students in Year 9 (aged 13–14 years) were highlighted and considered to be an important target group in a middle leaders' meeting. The deputy head teacher asked staff to make this group of 96 students the focus of their work. The school librarian, Kieran decided to look at the reading records for students in this group to identify those with low engagement, as this was his area of contact with them. He cross-referenced these records with the students' progress data in the academic monitoring system, to find those who had the lowest scores, resulting in a group of 23 students. He spoke to some of these students to gauge what he could offer that would motivate and support their progress in reading. Using Pupil Premium money, he devised an early morning reading group at whose meetings he provided tea and porridge, and he purchased multiple copies of some easy readers. The group developed into a shared reading project and the students knew that at the end of the project, if they completed four of the books provided, they would be invited to a cinema screening of a film they would like to see.

Ultimately Kieran created a spreadsheet with data on each student, listing his intervention and their progress. It showed a mixed picture: some students did not attend the reading group very often and some failed to complete the books, but others were more successful. The students with negative outcomes were identified as requiring further support and Kieran could describe their particular difficulties to senior leaders. Kieran contributed to the academic monitoring system in a way that demonstrated commitment and initiative, and by inference his project had an impact on the curriculum.

The next vignette illustrates the value of seizing informal opportunities to become involved in the assessment process. The new rules for exam access arrangements, which compel staff to gather detailed evidence of ongoing need over time, gave Jo such an opportunity.

School librarian Jo managed a very busy homework club after school and was assisted by some teaching assistants. One of the attendees was dyslexic and required substantial amounts of support from the team. New requirements were introduced for students who needed special access arrangements to be provided in public exams, e.g. the assistance of a reader or technology. In order for students to qualify for this access, staff needed to submit evidence about the level of regular support a student required when carrying out a task. Jo realized the homework club team was in an ideal position to contribute to this process and introduced a log for staff to note down students' names and the nature of support given without which they would not be able to complete a task. The academic monitoring team members were very pleased to receive the library's data, as building this evidence for applications for these special access arrangements for exams was proving to be a challenge.

This contribution shows how the library can support students with their learning both on a daily basis and for their longer-term welfare. A more formal involvement in assessment can entail many responsibilities and accountability for the learning outcomes achieved by students. To what extent and to what purpose should we get involved?

Caroline, a school librarian, wanted to contribute to the school's independent learning agenda, and proposed to her line manager that the more able Year 8 and 9 students should be allowed to work for the Higher

Project Qualification Level 2. This involved teaching them the skills they needed to carry out an independent research project, chosen by the individual students, and to assess their projects. The line manager agreed to Caroline's proposal. The students came to study skill classes once a week after school for 25 weeks, though some did not attend very often. Marking the projects gave Caroline valuable insights into the issues of assessment, and the pressures on teachers to produce results for an external qualification, as she had to analyse the assessment criteria and marking scheme, and apply it to the students' work. She was able to use her experience to improve the course for the next cohort, by starting earlier and increasing the amount of scaffold to support students. As a result a greater number of the students in the next year completed the project. After undertaking this work Caroline found that more teachers treated her as an equal.

School librarians need to exercise careful judgement when considering how far to become involved in the assessment process. Certainly it enriches one's knowledge and gives one greater cognitive authority in the eyes of teaching colleagues and students. However, being involved in assessment increases our workload considerably and we must make sure that we have time to carry out our other responsibilities.

When school librarians become part of the formal assessment and reporting system they are drawn into a pre-set programme with its attendant deadlines. This presents us with the same dilemmas as our teaching colleagues, who are also torn between what must be done to meet performance requirements and the things they believe should be done. When there is a conflict between meeting performance requirements and carrying out other tasks that we think are important it can be difficult to decide how to act. For example, there are benefits to including reading assessment in the academic monitoring system, because then the results are sent to parents in reports, but assessing reading levels for each student is very time consuming. It can lead to more clerical activity, for example data management, and less time interacting with the students. Re-considering how we think about our roles (see Chapter 1) may help us make decisions.

A more informal approach

Even if we do not engage fully with systematic evaluation we can still generate, select and use evidence in powerful ways to influence the viewpoints of others. We may collect or record the perceptions of others formally or informally, and feed them back to the head teacher, leadership members or line manager. For instance, a letter or e-mail from a parent or external body highlighting the positive aspects of the library's work can be used as evidence of impact, so it is important to circulate copies to relevant colleagues. Equally the perceptions of others can be cultivated. For instance, if a librarian sends an e-mail praising a colleague's work in the library to their head of department and the head teacher, it will create evidence for the teacher's performance review and is likely to foster that colleague's goodwill in future. It also demonstrates the type and quality of the work taking place in the library to the head teacher.

In the following vignette a librarian is under considerable pressure to demonstrate impact quickly.

Nargis was appointed to create a library in a new school. Her time was spent building the stock, organizing the room's layout and encouraging students to use the space at lunchtimes. After two months the head teacher expressed concern that he could not see any evidence of the librarian working with teachers or making a difference to students' literacy levels. After discussion with librarian colleagues Nargis realized that the value of processing stock was invisible and not the return on investment the head teacher envisaged. She re-prioritized some of her time so that she could audit the requirements of different departments and begin to host class visits. The other valuable tip Nargis received from other school librarians, which she immediately put into place, concerned display. She sought out student work that was reading or library-related from different departments and exhibited it in the library space. The head teacher could see a visible change in the library environment that made a clear link between its existence and work completed by students.

Another useful technique in our strategy to change people's perceptions could be to showcase the library's work, for example by creating a photo album of what happens in the library, or inviting the head teacher or a governor to visit some of the library's activities, such as seeing the reading club in action or presenting certificates to students in recognition of their successes. Involving the head teacher in celebrating the work of students in this way demonstrates that the library is successful and validates its role. This approach to celebrating student success in the library could be promulgated more widely; tutors could be asked to present certificates in class registrations, or certificates could be awarded in whole school assemblies. In these ways a positive attitude towards the library is created. These images give insights into the work of the library and enable others to form positive opinions, which they will feed into their evaluations of its role.

The place of benchmarking

Benchmarking is a process where we measure the quality of our policies, activities and outcomes against published standards or by using similar measurements made by our peers in other schools.

Benchmarking a library by collaborating with a peer in another school to compare practice in a chosen area enables us to examine differences and factors that underpin them. How far might these factors be open to change? Changing one factor in an area may enable practice to improve there. Trust and, to an extent, confidentiality are essential ingredients in this kind of process, because holding up the strengths, weaknesses and reasons behind an activity for detailed analysis by another can touch on sensitivities and local politics.

A number of school libraries in an area may wish to compare budget figures as part of a proposal for increased funding. Some data is politically sensitive and not all head teachers will support information sharing in this way. There may well be established guidelines on data use so we need to check before embarking on this type of exercise. Indeed, some library colleagues may not be comfortable about their data being made available beyond a conversation about benchmarking. We should remember that we need permission to use evidence that belongs to others.

We can gain valuable insights and challenge our assumptions by working closely with a neighbouring school library that has features in common (e.g. has the same state of development, is the same type and size of school) to conduct a peer review identifying differences in how a particular problem or service is managed. For example if we wanted to compare the amount of fiction borrowed from the libraries in two schools we might want to understand why the figure is higher in one school than in another. These are some reasons that might explain the discrepancy:

- One school has longer opening hours than the other or a larger budget for fiction.
- The librarian at one of the schools is a regular reader of new children's fiction and the other is not quite so keen.
- The philosophies of the English departments are different in nature.

- The schools have different activities to promote reading, and one is more popular than the other.
- There are differences in the schools' reader development programmes. If this is the case, why are they so?

Some factors that make a difference may be outside our influence, but it may be possible to affect others with some careful thought. Strategies for acquiring different perspectives are vital for future decision making because they help us to reduce our sense of parochialism and provide material for reports or discussion with our line manager.

Critical reflection

Generating and using evidence requires critical reflection. How do we make time for this? One method is to keep a learning journal or diary in which to note personal observations and the comments and thoughts of others at the end of a lesson or activity. Schon (1983) tells us that the reflective practitioner engages in both reflection in action and reflection on action. The first happens in the moment and is unconscious. The second happens later and is a more conscious process where we may discuss an experience with others before coming to a decision. It is essential to be critical when reflecting, to consider the matter from other perspectives. Four critical lenses have been suggested by Stephen Brookfield (1995, quoted in Gravells, 2014): our own point of view, that of our learners, that of our colleagues, and links with literature in order to compare our ideas with published theories. We can use the results of our critical thinking as valuable material to share with professional colleagues in social media forums, for instance in the form of a blog where the responses of others may flag up elements of the subject matter we had not previously considered.

A strategic approach to evaluation underpinned by careful reflection and shared with others ultimately makes the impact of a library on its school community clearer. As in many professional practices, the quality of critical thinking about school libraries improves if the practitioner is inspired. This takes us to Chapter 7.

P A R T   3

MOVING FORWARD

Inspiration

Do one thing every day that scares you.

Schmich, 2008

What is inspiration?

Inspiration can be a frightening word to use. It implies passion,
creativity, imagination and enthusiasm. To be inspired suggests being
endowed with vision and insight, having the confidence to take ideas
forward to action and perhaps transforming practice (e.g., Reynolds,
2008). People who are inspired brim with excitement and motivation
and are prepared to take risks. We believe that most of us have vast
potential; we can do extraordinary things if we have the confidence to
take risks.

Why is inspiration important to school librarianship?
A tale of two librarians

Annabel, a qualified librarian working in a high achieving girls' grammar
school, has a large library with a stock of around 15,000 volumes,
predominantly less than ten years old. She has had outstanding inspection

reports praising the use of the library by staff and students and the efficiency and professionalism with which she and her assistant run it. However the library is never mentioned in school publicity and Annabel does not engage in any activity outside the library – not even exchanging views with other librarians. Annabel feels comfortable in her work and she responds efficiently to requests. As the years pass Annabel continues to be very capable but finds it increasingly difficult to relate to the younger students. The library is still seen as a 'good thing' inside the school but the teachers don't stop to talk or think about it very much. When a new head teacher arrives and the budget is under pressure, the library is the first target to be looked at for cuts.

Saleha has worked in her school library for ten years. She is now increasingly conscious of the need to explore new possibilities and find inspiration in order to keep herself fresh and to drive the library forward. She wants to ensure that she maintains an identifiable place in her community. She has a well stocked, efficiently run library, which is fully used by staff and students alike; she feels that she has the respect of her colleagues. She enjoys her job but still she constantly looks for more. What drives this? Saleha believes that drawing inspiration from others, inside and outside the school, opens doors, enhances the way she works, and provides outlets for creativity. It gives her 'soul food', enthusiasm and passion that help generate new ideas and activities, satisfaction from others being motivated and inspired by her drive, and a rationale for her work. Her inspiration helps to reinforce, clarify and question the vision she has for the library, and as she feels inspired she has a better chance of motivating others to share in this belief.

These vignettes show two different ways of responding to our professional environment. Annabel was undoubtedly doing a 'good job' and was happy to continue her way of working within the school; Saleha is driven to find new ideas and approaches to inspire her work. Why should we bother to continually refresh ourselves? Does it make us better school librarians? Perhaps part of the answer lies in the nature of our professional context. Schools do not stand still. They adapt to the social environment; they implement waves of curriculum change; they integrate technological advances into teaching and learning; and they work to engage students whose concerns and enthusiasms change. In such an environment we need to challenge ourselves, our concept of our roles and our ways of fulfilling the job of school librarian. We cannot become too comfortable. We need to seek out inspiration.

Many of us feel that we lack the necessary creativity to enable us to come up with great new ideas or initiatives. However, inspiration does not have to come only from within ourselves. We can find illumination in all sorts of places. What is important is that we approach ideas with an open mind. We should be ready to act with an enthusiasm and energy that will enable us to apply those ideas that resonate with us to our own situations.

Having and implementing ideas is not the same as being inspired. Ideas can be safe and low key. They can take your practice forward gradually without disturbing or challenging your views or the views of others in your school. If there are problems you can back-pedal. Ideas are fundamental to good professional practice; being inspired adds an extra spark. Being inspired usually leads to risk taking and requires commitment and passion. Without inspiration we would never initiate fundamental changes in our practice, transform our professional understanding or fully inhabit our role of school librarian. It is as essential to the innovative school librarian as the air we breathe.

Most of us can recall inspirational teachers: those who stood out because they were quirky or loud or quietly passionate about their subject; those who grabbed and held our attention. These teachers must have taken risks to step away from ordinary practice and no doubt sometimes felt the criticism of their peers. They contrasted with colleagues who knew their subject well and delivered their topics with efficiency, but whose lessons were relatively mundane. An inspired person draws attention, makes people think and will in turn be able to inspire others. Becoming inspired is a risk worth taking; as Nehru is purported to have said, 'The policy of being too cautious is the greatest risk of all.'

We need determination and courage to take even relatively small risks.

Karen, a librarian in an independent school for 11–18 year olds, had struggled to keep the library silent during study time as instructed by her senior leadership team. She read an article in a library journal about the 'Mozart effect' and suggested at a teaching and learning committee meeting that she play classical music in the library. She argued that it might encourage a work ethic and calm the students. Some teachers were openly hostile to her idea but she persisted and was finally able to implement the change for a trial period, having carefully chosen the lessons during which she would play the music. Her high profile experiment was successful and some of those who had been sceptical were converted. One teacher even applied the idea in her laboratory practical sessions as a consequence.

When we decide to do something different in the library, we know that we may be in danger of distancing ourselves from the view of the majority. Many school librarians already feel that they work in isolation and are not truly accepted as members of the academic staff. Being creative can further upset the stability of our situations but we believe it is a risk worth taking to keep ourselves motivated, to inspire others and to improve the library's contribution to students' learning.

Sometimes we hear whispers in school that we are merely 'empire building', 'attention seeking' and 'deliberately stepping outside the box to provoke a reaction'. Change is unsettling for any organization and when it is instigated by an 'outsider' like the school librarian it may cause deep unrest. To combat this potential unease we can try to ensure that our ideas stand a very good chance of being successful while realizing that this may not happen. Careful management of change can help improve our chances of success. (See Chapter 9 for some ideas about this.) It is worth remembering that making significant changes may also be valued by the school, rather than criticized.

Catrin had introduced an independent learning course as an extra for the most able Year 9 students. While she had the enthusiastic support of her line manager, running the course was a considerable risk as it was the first time she had had to both teach and assess a whole course. She was particularly pleased to find that she was being consulted by teachers of the sixth form (16–18 year olds), who were considering introducing similar courses for their students and saw her as the expert. She was also able to discuss the possibility of introducing an independent learning project for a larger number of the Year 9 students.

How does inspiration operate?

Inspiration can be pushed forward on many levels within a school. Options range from exploring an idea with a single member of teaching staff (which may, if successful, then be taken up by others in that department), to going directly to the senior leadership team with an idea for adoption across the school. Inspiration can begin small, based in a personal enthusiasm or an idea for one particular area of practice without a clear view of where it might lead.

Jan, a librarian in a school with 13–18-year-old pupils, set up a wiki for her staff book group. She motivated the group members by talking enthusiastically about the potential of this new form of collaboration and encouraged them to think about other applications. One of the book club members, Lynn, also attended regular academic support group meetings with Jan. Two months later, having been reminded about the book club wiki, and discovering that she could create group project pages, Lynn was inspired to set up a similar site for this academic committee. In particular, she could see the value of using this tool as a form of communication between meetings.

It matters not whether being inspired takes the shape of a small or large endeavour. We might want to enact sweeping changes or envision one new initiative that is fundamental to achieving the school's goals. Inspiration may also come as an intuition, an insight into why something is the way it is, leading to affirmation of an existing approach or to deeper understanding of the barriers to change. We can control the level of risk and change that we engage with, as long as we continue to seek inspiration and the influx of creativity that accompanies it.

For long-term influence and effectiveness perhaps a blend of work at all levels is needed. If we only collaborate with certain individuals our work may become fragmented and we may be viewed as 'unapproachable' by those outside our charmed circle. If we focus our efforts on the school leadership we may miss the opportunity to make a real impact on individual staff and students in the shorter term. To get a good balance it may be useful to think about inspiration at two levels: the operational level (new things to do with students and staff to engage and motivate them), and the strategic level (new roles and directions – a whole new vision for the school library that may involve a re-evaluation of our values and the way we approach our job).

The operational level

Marianne, a school librarian in a small, mixed, inner-city school, was faced with a large number of students who entered school with low reading ages and little interest in reading. She had previously tried to engage students in reading by shadowing the Carnegie Award for children's literature in the UK. However she was increasingly worried that the books were not appropriate for her students and that this strategy was having little impact on their reading. She then read a piece of research that criticized passive activities (such as shadowing big events and arranging author visits) to promote reading (Todd, 2005a). This prompted Marianne to find out more about participative events and to talk to librarians at other schools. She was inspired to develop a new and more adventurous reading project with three other local schools: setting up their own book award. This award generated high levels of interest and resulted in Marianne's students reading more widely.

The strategic level

Eric was the librarian in a large, mixed inner-city school. His school was working hard to improve communication with its feeder primary schools. Eric contributed to the transitions programme by giving talks to groups of the primary school children in the term before they were due to start at his school by teaching them about the library layout and how to use the online catalogue. Informal discussions with colleagues and primary school teachers got him thinking more about supporting students' transition between primary and secondary school. Eric wondered whether teaching catalogue skills and giving information was the best way of enabling these children to cope when they came to the secondary school. He tried out a number of different strategies, including peer teaching, collaborative group work, pairing with older students and facilitating extended activities involving parents and community groups, such as a world history event. Eric found that reconnecting with his belief in enabling learning gave him the impetus to re-invent his practice and not just with the new students. He found himself changing the ways in which he interacted with students throughout the school, doing less telling and teaching and more supporting.

How do we keep ourselves inspired?

We can all open ourselves up and be ready for inspiration but where do we find it? In the preceding vignettes the school librarians used colleagues and reading to stay creative. Is this enough? Unlike air, inspiration is not all around us; we may have to seek it out.

Jane and Philippa, librarians at two different schools, attended a large information literacy conference and heard a presentation on plagiarism. The dynamism, passion and enthusiasm of the speaker struck a chord. They both realized how little recognition this important issue had been given in their schools to date. Fired with enthusiasm they returned with a resolve to raise the profile of issues surrounding plagiarism in their schools. They approached this in two different ways. Jane reported back to members of the senior leadership team, who asked her to produce a draft school policy. She also developed a teaching unit on academic honesty to be delivered to students, either by herself or teachers. This led to greater recognition of her role within the teaching and learning of the school. Philippa was emboldened to suggest to her senior leadership team that they should invite the conference speaker to the school to speak directly to the staff and sixth form students.

How we act on inspiration is the critical factor for the impact it will have.

Inspiration for us, in our jobs as school librarians, is about professional learning. How do we learn? Formal training and educational qualifications, professional reading materials and networking with each other are tangible ways of learning and gaining inspiration. At a deeper level getting and using inspiration is about us as individual learners. To view professional learning as a matter of acquiring a certain set of skills and knowledge is to take a technical-rational approach. This does not allow for individual differences in development and interpretation, which are the reality in every school library. We can all attend the same course but what we take from it depends on our prior understanding, which determines what makes sense to us and what seems compatible with our library setting. (An overview of professional development opportunities in the UK can be found in Shaper, 2014.)

Real professional learning is a process that is personal and unique. We make connections between what we already know and the new. We form a deep link to an idea as a result of our professional context, personal values and individual understanding of our role. We then draw the idea in, re-shaping it and making it our own. This process enables us to re-conceptualize our practice, views and philosophy. Many inspirational ideas are sparked through conversations with work colleagues. Discussing topical issues with others can help us make connections and see openings for a different approach to a problem or where to try a new idea. The continuing struggle to make sense of the new, to create new knowledge and understanding, is what drives professional practice.

How do we each learn most effectively? Do we benefit most from formal study, research, reflecting on models, working with mentors, discussion with colleagues, trial and error, or observation of students, teachers, librarians and others? Perhaps some or all of these are helpful at different times?

As we discussed in Chapter 2 school librarians are frequently solo practitioners and can become professionally isolated – and isolation is often the enemy of inspiration. Isolation can make all ideas, however good, seem like impossible dreams. It is then easy for the librarian to take refuge in the day-to-day routines that keep us busy, but are not creative or developmental.

So, how do we keep ourselves motivated and full of fresh insights or, in other words, inspired? We should begin by recognizing that inspiration comes in many guises and from many sources; it is sometimes desperately sought and at other times quite unexpected in its arrival.

Inspiration from inside ourselves

Inspiration can be stimulated by critical reflection. However we need to do more than merely reflect on specific instances of our practice, considering technical questions such as how to 'tweak' a lesson or improve the delivery of a service. This is good professional practice and can be motivating, but is unlikely to inspire. We need to go further and examine our values and assumptions.

Reflecting on what we do is essential to the development of professional judgement, but unless our reflection involves some form of challenge to, and critique of, ourselves and our professional values we tend simply to reinforce existing patterns and tendencies (Tripp, 1993).

Critical reflection helps us to understand and connect with the energy that we need to perform our roles as school librarians. Evidence of impact helps determine our priorities for practice and identify sources of inspiration.

Sometimes in the face of difficulties we look to our values for personal inspiration. These are deeply rooted; they form part of our identity and underpin our actions. They shape our philosophy and vision for practice, as was discussed in some depth in Chapter 1, but can take a back seat in the face of the everyday demands made on us to keep the school library working. They need to be consciously revisited and re-polished to provide a source of strength. A mixture of vision (values translated into practice), enthusiasm and passion leads to inspiration.

In addition we must believe in ourselves and the potential impact of what we do:

> We too often undersell the importance and raw power of what we do.
> We are a noble profession. We don't shelve books, and change toner
> cartridges – we maintain an infrastructure for social action. We don't
> reference resources, and catalog artifacts – we teach and inspire . . .
> librarians can overcome the crushing forces of mediocrity and cynicism
> – but we must believe that we can. . . . This is what inspires me.
>
> Lankes, 2009

However, it is difficult for us to draw continually on our inner strengths for inspiration. We can keep ourselves motivated by asking for feedback, finding out where we have made a difference, and evaluating our contribution to the school. But in order to move beyond motivation into inspiration, we often need to look outside ourselves.

Inspiration from inside the school

Sometimes the school itself can provide inspiration through programmes it may already be running or introducing. An inspirational initiative can enthuse us to be imaginative, to develop the ways in which the special resources of the library and our skills can give added value to the school: in other words, to respond positively to the school's needs.

An English teacher came to Alice, a school librarian in an inner-city girls' school, with the idea of 'doing something with storytelling'. She had no clear goal in mind, just a desire to motivate the students. Alice and the teacher started to explore the possibilities and their collaboration gave strong momentum to the idea. They became more adventurous than either would have been on their own and decided to take students to perform at an international storytelling festival. Alice worked with the students to help them find and develop their stories, gave them opportunities to perform to their peers in the library, and organized their visits to other schools and festivals. The joint initiative became a prizewinning success.

We need to identify and engage with work colleagues who are positive in their attitude and on whom we can rely to give moral support and an honest, unbiased opinion. In each school there are people who are particularly active, who have a 'can do' approach to life. Collaborating with them or even talking to them is likely to keep us feeling positive and so more open to inspiration. Otherwise we may fall short of the vision we are proposing:

> As I go around the country I encounter too many librarians who see the vision, who embrace change, but have grown too tired and discouraged to hope again. They are quieted by the scars of past optimism. . . . It may sound simplistic, but for me it comes down to needing some encouragement. We need to know that we are not alone.
>
> Lankes, 2009

Inspiration from outside the school

Fellow library professionals can be a good source of inspiration, but to maintain contact with such colleagues we need to set up regular, preferably frequent, visits to other schools. Continuous professional development activities, such as the courses provided by our professional associations and others, are a prime source of inspiration, which need to be supplemented by more informal contact with our colleagues. It is noteworthy that the school library professions in the USA, Australia and the UK have all developed e-mail lists enabling them to exchange views, ideas and information, often joined by professionals from other parts of the world.

We also need to maintain a genuinely open and curious mindset and be prepared to be inspired. It is easy to slip into a 'that won't work in my school' mentality; to dismiss different practice because it is in a school context that is not like our own – one with more resources, different types of students, a bigger library or a different curriculum – or even in a non-school environment. We need to develop ways of seeing that enable us to look beyond the surface to the possibilities beneath. The key is not to skip over something written by a law librarian simply because we cannot directly transfer the ideas to our school. We need to stay alert to the possibilities inherent in all situations, to make connections and think laterally. Otherwise we are simply making excuses for inaction.

Susan saw a television programme on the radical redesign of everyday objects that made her wonder if she automatically assumed she should deliver a particular portfolio of activities in a particular way. She recalled a conversation with a science teacher about the most effective balance between laboratory and classroom teaching. She began to question whether she should find ways of supporting the initial stages of student research in the classroom rather than the library. She developed units of work to outline research strategies and methods that encouraged students to think about their research questions and define the areas they needed to explore before their first visits to the library.

We may also learn from colleagues who are inspirational within their own contexts even if these are different from our own. We might examine their values and goals, watch how they achieve their results, and consider which elements we might adapt. We should not be afraid to ask questions so that we understand what influences their decisions and what vision drives their practice. The wider our networks, the more likely we are to chance on some opportunity for inspiration or to hear something that challenges our thinking or assumptions.

One great advantage we have over some other areas of librarianship is that we are directly involved with learning, perhaps one of the most intrinsically inspiring of human activities. We are concerned with both knowledge and skills, so we can connect with all parts of the curriculum in one form or another, as well as with overarching capabilities such as information literacy and thinking skills. Then we can look to a wide range of programmes and professionals for inspiration.

Lynn's school was trying to develop an effective reading culture within the school where all the students were able to see reading as a source of pleasure. Dyslexia and other problems with literacy had increasingly been recognized by staff in Lynn's school as a significant barrier to progress for many children. Reading for pleasure often seemed impossible for these children. She researched the issue on websites and blogs concerned with library-based literacy initiatives, and was inspired by a blog post on using digital technology to encourage students who did not enjoy reading. She was able to buy a number of tablets with reading apps and work with the learning support department to develop their use.

Lynn moved beyond the traditional text sources of information on resources for dyslexics, which in turn led her to less traditional ways of supporting them.

Initial education in librarianship provides the bedrock for our everyday practice but it will not keep us inspired. It is ongoing professional learning that provides a wellspring for inspiration. There are many formal opportunities open to school librarians who want to continue to learn: professional bodies offer relevant and interesting courses and workshops on aspects of librarianship and facets of teaching; university departments of librarianship and information studies offer accredited programmes; and courses designed for teachers, both in school and out, are often extremely valuable.

Seeing things from the teacher's perspective can be inspirational; it can change the way we think about the role of the library and develop our vision of how it can support teaching and learning. Insight into teachers' values and beliefs may stimulate us to re-examine our own. In addition, new theoretical constructs about learning and how it manifests itself may inspire us to change our approach. As well as learning from the inspirational content of any course we may also learn from the processes encountered. Being a learner in a formal situation can remind us about emotional aspects of learning and enable us to discuss learning with students and teachers in a more focused and informed manner.

Inspiration can emerge from a range of formal learning opportunities but its emergence hinges on how we approach these opportunities. An open mind coupled with genuine curiosity is most likely to lead to inspiration.

What has inspired us?

The range of possibilities that we have discussed for obtaining inspiration shows how widely we can cast our nets in our efforts to stay creative, enthusiastic and motivated. This was emphasized when we stopped to consider what had inspired us to become school librarians and what kept us inspired in that role. Each of us had a different story:

- I was 17 and had secured a place on a teacher-training course when I got a Saturday job at my local public library and was trained and nurtured by the branch librarian. I loved working with the public and, yes, stamping books, but she took me to book selection meetings and out with the housebound service, and involved me in running the holiday club as well. She had a clear vision and sense of purpose and was the very model of someone who exemplified the 'service ethic'. I wanted to be like her.

- I was a good library manager but when I went on a one-day course about the effective school library I was changed, in one day, into a more reflective practitioner, something that I had never thought about before. Not only did I learn how to ask questions of myself and about my service but for the first time I began to think that maybe I, too, could do a masters' degree.

- My inspiration began with a special needs teacher in junior school who took me out of lessons and, over a space of three years, taught me to read and boosted my confidence immensely by saying that nothing could stop me now and that I just needed to read as many books as possible. I realized a few years ago that life had moved full circle as I now work closely with young people who need help to develop their reading skills. Nothing gives me greater inspiration or satisfaction than seeing them break through those personal barriers.

- I was first inspired to become a librarian by my husband's problems in finding the information he needed for a business venture; his difficulties brought home to me the importance of information accessibility, and the idea that I might help to do something about it. Since then I have been repeatedly enthused and inspired by other practitioners and a multitude of training courses. Networking has been a vital part of keeping inspired.

- I discovered information science by accident as an alternative to laboratory work and my career has included pharmaceutical market research and financial libraries. Being a school librarian inspires me because of the opportunities it gives for altruism. I love sharing ideas, passing information on to others and watching them learn, develop and create as a result.

- Having worked in university, public and government libraries I took a part-time job as a school librarian after a career break. Realizing that I needed to retrain, I seized every opportunity to visit other school libraries. A School Library Association meeting for new school librarians provided the inspiration I needed to embark on a masters' degree in education. School librarianship continues to absorb and inspire me with the various challenges and potential for creativity it presents.

Reality check

We must be careful not to let inspiration result in frustration, disappointment and ultimately even demoralization, which can happen if we focus on what is unattainable. Before we invest too much energy in a new idea, vision or belief, we should consider our inspiration in the context of the bigger picture – the overall aims of both the school and the library. This will determine which ideas are doable and which are not.

Sharing inspiration

Just as we have gained inspiration from others, it is important that we in turn pass on what we have done. This may take a whole variety of forms, through:

- informal reporting back to groups of local librarians
- writing, for example on an e-mail list for school librarians, articles

for the professional or educational press, whether for school librarians or the wider library community, professional blogs, on social media, papers for conferences, reports in the local or even national press
- reaching out to teachers and head teachers.

Whatever the forum, it is important to aim to do more than simply report on our activities, if we wish others to draw on our experiences and use them to improve our practice.

This can appear even more daunting than keeping ourselves inspired. The extent to which it is possible for us to inspire others will depend on the vision, passion and enthusiasm we convey; the effectiveness with which we carry out our ideas; and the quality of our connections to, and communication with, others. It will also depend on the image we have of ourselves and our role in the school. Do we see ourselves in a supporting role or as leaders of learning? Supporters follow others and do not usually inspire. Leaders of learning make things happen. They experiment with practice; they gather and use evidence to make a difference to student learning; they collaborate to influence and encourage change; they model particular approaches (Todd, 2005b). 'It is difficult to be seen as a leader if you do not behave like one and are not seen with other leaders' (Webb, 2012).

Inspiration also goes beyond networking and sharing experiences – the traditional strengths of the school librarian. It is important to ask who we talk to about our work, ideas and values, but we also need to ask how we can enable others to adapt our ideas to suit their contexts and styles, to be inspired enough to grow their own projects.

Thomas's attention was caught by proposals for a professional development day on digital technology for teachers in his school. It was being designed to 'spice up' teaching with wikis, blogs, podcasts and other tools. He had experimented with Diigo and found it a useful way to gather URLs together and organize them for others to access. He approached the head of IT who was co-ordinating the day and asked whether anything was planned on social bookmarking, as he thought it would help students to find and organize information. The head of IT admitted that she was not familiar with social bookmarking but liked the possible practical applications of the software. She invited Thomas to demonstrate it to the staff. Thomas felt this was outside his comfort zone as the day was all about teaching strategies used in the classroom. However, he could see the value of contributing to a course that was so central to teachers' concerns. Thomas made sure that he discussed the applications of social bookmarking to teaching and learning with the head of IT before he planned the session where he demonstrated how he had used it, and the benefits for both teachers and students.

People watch what we do more than they listen to what we say. We all need to ask ourselves what aspects of our practice might inspire someone else and how we can build on that.

Does inspiring others mean that we have to be outgoing, to stand out from the crowd, to stick our heads above the parapet? Certainly in some situations we may need to project a passionate and enthusiastic persona. It may be necessary to challenge the status quo, confound expectations and ask difficult questions in order to find an alternative route to achievement or to prod colleagues into change. Some librarians definitely inspire from the front – and enjoy it!

School librarian Judith is very conscious of her role in inspiring colleagues. She says, 'They have grown to trust me. If they see that I can ask questions without retribution but gaining respect, it inspires them to follow my example and ultimately change for the better can be achieved. It is important to become a "voice" within the workplace community. However, I am aware that what I do, say and promise has to be backed by practical results.'

However, speaking out in a community is not the only way to motivate others. We can inspire others via the quiet discussion of new ideas, the demonstration of something in action that initially aroused only scepticism, or through a genuine and sustained interest in how our students think, feel and learn. Every librarian with vision is capable of inspiring others.

How wide should we spread our net? The most effective librarians do not rely on motivating just one segment of the community.

Marie, who was already proactive in promoting reading for pleasure in her school, was inspired by Cityread London (www.cityread.london) to try to get everyone associated with her school to read the same book – not just the students and staff but also governors and parents. She could see that because it would be a considerable challenge it would also be a real achievement if she initiated such a project. Not being a very outgoing sort of character she quietly enlisted a few key allies among the teachers and held a short meeting to discuss how to get the idea off the ground. So it developed into a group project, which really helped it to take off.

Whichever road we follow, we must remember that inspiring others is not the same as informing them. We need to go beyond imparting ideas, demonstrating practice and merely presenting the evidence. For example, school librarians have spent a great deal of time trying to communicate what we mean by information literacy. In our endeavours to overcome the barrier that language and its meanings pose, we repeatedly design models to show not only teachers but also each other what we mean by information literacy. We use reification, objectify and attempt to make a learning process tangible. We have some success in sharing our ideas. Yet it is in the practice of working closely with a teaching colleague that we achieve joint understanding (Wenger, 1998).

When collaborating we go beyond informing. When we begin we are conscious that we are all in different places in our understanding of a topic, but gradually meanings are negotiated and new learning evolves. Then, at some point, inspiration occurs. It is a dynamic process that depends on genuine engagement with other people.

We could be seen to ignore our own strictures by writing this book, since it informs rather than builds participation, collaboration and shared meanings. However, we believe that in sharing our values and our vision, as well as examples of these in practice, we are taking a positive step forward. We also recognize the need to take this type of communication into other arenas. As individuals we must talk to those entering the profession to promote this specialized area of education librarianship. As individuals and groups we must project our identity and role within the teaching and learning process into the consciousness of head teachers and future head teachers.

> We need the inspiration and hope to keep us moving forward and improving even in hard times. . . . Inspiration is something you have to search for. Don't wait for it, search for it. And when you find it, embrace it, and don't let anyone take it from you. . . . Don't underestimate the value of inspiration and do not apologise for becoming profoundly inspired or in inspiring others. . . . Inspiration is not everything – you need great ideas, action and hard work too – but genuine learning and growth and real change come to those who are inspired.
>
> Reynolds, 2008

CHAPTER 8

Becoming integral to teaching and learning

We believe that becoming an integral part of the teaching and learning process is an important goal for school librarians. However, in the literature of school librarianship, and indeed the whole field of librarianship, integration is presented as the Utopia, which implies that we may aspire to but never achieve it. We believe, on the contrary, that becoming integral to teaching and learning within schools is not only a valid aspiration for school librarians but achievable. It is the process of working together with members of our school community to achieve integration that gives real purpose to our work.

Integration is also the process whereby the librarian and the library become essential parts of the school at all levels. As we have said already, this is part of serving the community in which we work, a core part of any librarian's role. Becoming integrated involves:

- looking at structure and staffing
- considering where the librarian sits within the internal management of the school
- making constructive relationships within the school community
- thinking about the place the library and the librarian occupy within teaching and learning

- working to be a visible part of the solution to the students'
  learning needs.   (Streatfield and Markless, 1994)

We recognize that integration may take place at different points along a continuum from working with an individual teacher to whole school involvement. Levels of integration fluctuate over time, as the school's management structure, curriculum and personnel change.

Although our aim of supporting the core purposes of the organization should be constant, we need to determine what form integration might take according to context.

We each need to build a vision of what integration looks like in our workplace. There will be a range of possibilities, which need to be linked to the librarian's capabilities, opportunities and aspirations to create a dynamic response to the teaching and learning culture of the school.

How, then, do we achieve integration with the rest of the school? It can be done in any of the following ways:

- through becoming an integral part of the teaching team
- through forging constructive relationships
- by sustaining integration into teaching and learning
- by being innovative with physical and virtual library space
- by using the virtual library
- by playing a role in the management of the school.

Opportunities may arise in all of these areas, which we will now explore. To be effective we need to consider how we get involved, what effect our involvement has on teaching and learning, and how we sustain that level of participation.

Becoming an integral part of the teaching team

Where the library is truly successful it becomes so through the librarian making clearly visible contributions to teaching and learning, which are recognized and valued. As a result we are identified with core activities, come to have value in the eyes of teachers, and are seen as part of the same team.

The classic approach to achieving integration of the school library is to concentrate on bringing teachers to the library but, as Chapter 5 has shown, it is necessary to reach out in many different ways. We can become important to the work of teachers through providing experiences for students that enable them to learn effectively in a variety of locations, thus helping teachers meet their priorities.

Sam is a school librarian in a school that has a well established teaching and learning group, which is highly thought of by senior leaders; its ideas regularly feed into the school improvement plan. The group's new leader announced that he was keen to start a teaching and learning blog so that staff could share ideas and discuss issues. However, lack of time and confidence meant that colleagues were reluctant to post items and so it was slow to get started. Despite her lack of experience with blogging, Sam decided that this was a good opportunity to show her support for the teaching and learning group and demonstrate her relevance to their agenda. So, she wrote a piece about the problems of promoting wider reading. It led to a new rapport with the grateful group leader and sparked an interesting debate with colleagues on a topic of great importance to the library.

Understanding the curriculum in its broadest sense is vital. In the UK, this used to be fairly straight forward as there was a centrally imposed national curriculum. However, many secondary schools such as academies, free schools and independent schools – now the majority of schools in England and Wales – are not bound by this document (Department for Education, 2014b; Roberts, 2014). This fragmentation makes it imperative for school librarians to find out our school's curriculum and our teachers' choices of examination board options.

Using this knowledge of the curriculum, our contribution to teaching and learning can range from working with whole classes alongside a classroom teacher, to supporting individual students with extended essays, independent projects and coursework. Every change to the National Curriculum offers us an opportunity. For example in England replacing ICT courses (which tended to be narrowly interpreted) with computing (which is treated more inclusively) gives us the chance to develop our role as key players in the field of information literacy, digital literacy and independent learning.

Similarly, interest in enquiry-based learning (Wellcome Trust, 2011), and discussions about how the curriculum can be adapted to include this, gives us a useful opportunity to support teachers in ways that they will appreciate. We also know that information literacy skills are vital to students. Universities around the world are laying more and more emphasis on the ability to carry out research: 'Universities have welcomed the extended project to be offered as part of A Levels and Diplomas because it gives students the research, critical thinking and evaluation skills they value' (Department for Children, Schools and Families, 2008).

The earlier students acquire these skills, the more likely they are to absorb and adapt them into their practice, and the more able they will be to meet future demands. It is now up to us to seize this opportunity to integrate our knowledge and expertise to help teachers teach this new extended curriculum. This has the potential to demonstrate the convergence of our interests as information specialists with those of teachers and the school more generally.

Changes in the curriculum inevitably lead to changes in pedagogy. For example an increasing emphasis on independent learning has led some schools to adopt the 'flipped classroom' method of teaching (Nottingham Trent University, 2013), in which students prepare in advance for a lesson, changing their role from passive recipient to active participant. The teacher role then becomes that of facilitator and monitor of learning. In this scenario we can seize opportunities to offer guidance, help and support with developing good research techniques and to provide appropriate resources, and so become involved in the teaching and learning process. Supplying this support may be important because this style of learning does not suit everyone; for example those on the autistic spectrum may need a more structured approach.

These examples taken together demonstrate the depth of understanding we need about the curriculum and its associated pedagogies if we are to make the most of our opportunities and thus become integrated.

The following vignette illustrates the circle of participation, inclusion, engagement and learning.

James received a letter from a parent complaining that their child had simply copied and pasted their science homework. James showed it to the science teacher who admitted that most of her Year 8 class had seemed to have done the same. Together they planned a lesson to help these students realize the importance of academic honesty and writing in their own words. James constructed an essay with obvious signs of being copied and this was displayed to students on a whiteboard. The students were asked to comment on what was wrong and unacceptable.

The students then peer marked the original homework and wrote on a card three positive comments and three comments on areas that needed improvement. They then handed back the homework and cards to the author.

The students were shocked by the results, which showed the extent of their plagiarism. James was given the opportunity to teach the class how to research, write effectively and reference their work, while the teacher outlined the subject content expected for their next assignment. This lesson took place in the classroom and was followed by a research session in the library. James awarded marks as part of the final assessment for the skills that he had taught.

The teacher was pleased with the improvement in written work and incorporated James' involvement into her scheme of work for this topic. By working closely with the teacher and class in this way, James began to build a stronger relationship with them.

Forging constructive relationships

Without the development of successful pedagogic relationships with teachers and students, we run the real risk of being at the periphery of the main work of teaching and learning in the school where we work. Relationship building is a learning process. A school's activities and success depend on the strength of its relationships and the ability of staff to continue as learners. What makes a teacher a good teacher is their continuing desire to find out what works best for learners. If we wish to integrate, then we must be partners in this process, questioning our assumptions to tackle this challenge. This requires working with teachers to develop joint meanings and understandings of learning and what we want our students to be able to do.

Ross Todd (2005b) challenges school librarians to consider how we move students forward. He suggests that we should want them to be able to:

- search actively for meaning and understanding

- construct deep knowledge and understanding rather than passively receiving it
- be directly involved and engaged in the discovery of new knowledge rather than collecting facts and data
- encounter alternative perspectives and conflicting ideas so they can transform prior knowledge and experience into deep understandings
- transfer new knowledge and skills to new circumstances
- use a range of complex knowledge construction competencies to transform raw data, prior knowledge and information into deep understanding
- take ownership and responsibility for their ongoing learning and mastery of curriculum content and skills
- contribute to societal well-being, the growth of democracy, and the development of a knowledgeable society.

This will only happen if we collaborate with teachers.

We can also build relationships through cross-curricular activities. Organizing school-based activities, such as author visits and poetry workshops, can be beneficial in raising our profile and more importantly increasing the cultural enrichment of students. However, standalone activities are not of themselves a force for integration and may even run counter to it.

Some years ago Pat had spotted an offer giving a free Ordnance Survey local area map to each Year 7 pupil. She registered her school but, to her disappointment, over the years dealing with the administration of this the initiative just became a chore for the library with no real benefit. The geography teachers did not even want to bring their classes to the library to receive their maps let alone collaborate as a result. So, when the Book Trust announced their Book Buzz scheme, which gave a subsidized reading book to every Year 7 pupil, Pat thought hard about how to make more of this opportunity. She signed up for the scheme, invested from the library budget, and undertook the administration involved. She also spoke to the English teachers who allowed her class time to talk about the books on offer so that students could make an informed choice. When the books arrived the English teachers helped to make it a special occasion when they brought their classes to collect the books. Then, sometime later a two-day event was held which explored the books through drama workshops, deepening the students' understanding of character and theme.

This is an example of an area where the librarian was already involved but needed to change her approach. Working with teachers and becoming integral to teaching and learning may be a step further than we are used to, but will pay dividends in encouraging teachers to recognize the contribution we make.

Cross-curricular activities offer other possibilities for us to demonstrate that we are an integral part of the school's teaching and learning. For example, a whole school themed day offers good opportunities for library involvement. Where these take place, schools need to produce evidence of their impact on students' motivation and learning. We should be a part of the team producing that evidence, so it is important to seek feedback from both students and teachers.

Sustaining integration into teaching and learning

The process of integration needs continuous nurturing, as teachers and curricula change. Faced with the need to absorb curricular change into their practice, even the most well disposed teacher may slip back into seeing the librarian as an information resource rather than integral to the teaching and learning process.

Olivia was included in the discussions for creating a special curriculum for the bottom set in Year 7, involving theme-based cross-curricular work rather than discrete subject teaching. The head of Year 7 spoke warmly of the contribution she would be making as a knowledgeable source of materials to support the teachers, rather than as a potential co-developer and teaching partner. Olivia could see that this was a good starting point, but that she would need to work hard to develop good quality learning experiences. So she volunteered to help with writing assessment criteria for the skills element of the curriculum and promoted a way of helping students engage with information in a process of 'mediation'

(Williams and Wavell, 2006a).

This example of high level partnership with one or more teachers shows how the librarian and teachers worked closely to develop a unit of work and teach together as a team. They could so easily have worked much less effectively. A school culture that capitalizes on the librarian in this way makes the best possible use of their investment. Where we are successful in developing and teaching units of work alongside teachers, we will be more valued.

Being innovative with library space

When we consider how we make effective use of our libraries we need to think about both physical and virtual environments and how these overlap.

Despite the need to reach out, it is important to remember that the library traditionally has been first and foremost a physical space, housing physical resources. This was a significant part of its function, and will continue to be the main way that libraries are perceived by many teachers, students, parents and leaders of education. But rapid advances in technology such as e-books, apps and social media have radically altered the way we access information and read. Today's school libraries have adapted their physical space to accommodate these changes.

Louisa had a traditional library dominated by fixed shelves and a library desk with poor sight lines. A new head decided to prioritize upgrading the library to increase its use. The vision was of an open space with modern technology placed at the forefront of teaching and learning.

Louisa researched how she could effect this transformation and still retain a balance between physical and online resources. She decided to replace some of the old stock with digital books, and to reduce the amount of shelving and replace it with mobile bookcases. She realized that the availability of Wi-Fi together with the school's bring your own device initiative reduced the need for fixed computer desks.

She worked with the design team to ensure there were discrete zones for different study styles, for example a silent space for private study, an area for collaborative learning, and a soft seating area to encourage reading. The library desk was made central. She even considered a 'makerspace' (Loertscher, 2013) to encourage practical creativity.

These innovative changes had a direct effect on the use of the library in the way the head had envisaged. More students engaged with the facilities on offer by visiting the library and using the online resources. The new facilities and services inspired teachers to explore fresh ways of using the librarian.

Using the virtual library to enhance integration

A recent survey commissioned by Google suggests that today's teenagers rely on information targeted to them by online services: 'I would say nine times out of 10, almost 10 times out of 10, if I'm watching video content online, it's because somebody has pushed it to me' (Think Newsletter, 2013).

Are we in a true era of 'libraries without walls' (Brophy, Craven and Markland, 2008)? Even though pupils may not visit the library in person we can provide a virtual service. Our students can also access a variety of online resources 24/7 from public libraries (e.g. Surrey Library Services, http://new.surreycc.gov.uk/people-and-community/libraries).

Technological change offers us new ways to integrate. Many school libraries now have social media accounts through which they promote their resources and activities. Use of social bookmarking sites can demonstrate our ability to support teaching and learning. Some librarians organize their school's virtual learning environment (VLE) or portal. By developing activities for students that make use of the VLE system, we can underline the learning potential of the library. But to achieve integration we need to go beyond a 'library page' to embedding the library throughout the VLE, for example by creating a link to the online public access catalogue from every department page; showing relevant library and external resources; giving advice on bibliographies, citation and plagiarism; and reminding users about information literacy. Mobile technology applications can also be developed and most library catalogues are available 24/7, further endorsing the idea that libraries have no walls. Similarly e-books and audio books can be promoted and read at the touch of a button. At present the opportunities for use of mobile technology may be limited through constrictions of broadband width, Wi-Fi availability and the school's restrictions on the use of devices in class. We might decide to take the initiative to become involved in teaching digital literacy and online safety, ensuring that the technology is being used to solve a problem rather than being a gimmick with little impact on teaching and learning.

Building into the structure and management of the school

The range of abilities and attitudes Todd (2005a) wrote about (listed in the section 'Forging constructive relationships', above) cannot be delivered without school librarians being integrated into teaching and learning. If we accept that the aspirations Todd proposed are valid we need to look at ways to sell them to our school, and offer concrete paths through which to make them tangible. The ways to do this vary. We each need to involve ourselves in how our schools approach teaching and learning so that we are equipped to incorporate our aspirations into those of the school.

One of the most important steps the librarian can take is to become included in the school's academic structure. This is partly a matter of function, to be seen as playing a role in the academic management of the school. The UK libraries' professional body CILIP recommends that school librarians are ranked with middle leaders as heads of department and this status enables us to have influence (CILIP, 2014b).

However, some of us find that inclusion at the level of middle leadership is still a goal rather than a reality, and earning it may depend more on the mindset of senior leadership than on our abilities or contribution. Nonetheless, achieving this integration should be our aim, because without it we are excluded from many of the discussions that affect how and to what extent we can contribute to the work of the school. Whether these discussions take place at heads of department meetings or within specifically academic groups such as a teaching and learning committee is not important. The vital thing is to be included in the discussions about the delivery of the school's core aim, otherwise we may simply be invisible to those planning the future of the school.

How do we convince those in the senior leadership team that we can make a greater contribution to the work of the school from within middle leadership than from without? We may follow the example of one school librarian who with a mixture of luck and nerve was able to be accepted as a full member of the middle leadership team.

Jane, a new school librarian, turned up at heads of department meetings – from which her predecessor had been excluded. The deputy head who normally chaired was off that term on sick-leave. He queried her presence on his return, saying he thought she would not find it relevant. When she said that she had found it useful by allowing her to focus library buying on new courses and to build a number of partnerships with department heads, he agreed to her continued attendance.

Getting included is seldom so simple. A librarian already in a school and not in the habit of being included in heads of departments' meetings will probably need to justify attending by arguing the need to be aware of school curriculum discussions and the school priorities. Other opportunities to get ourselves noticed might arise from the importance now attached to literacy and independent learning and the need to show value for money.

Participating in in-service training (INSET) might also be valuable. For example, if a school decides to experiment with in-house INSET as part of its continuing professional development programme we might take the opportunity to offer a session on academic honesty, particularly if plagiarism has been identified as a growing concern and teachers are uncertain about how to tackle it.

We need to remember that integration within the school goes beyond its management structure. There are social aspects of integration, which include taking part in school events and building relationships with other school staff. These were dealt with in more depth in Chapter 5.

We have explored the wide variety of opportunities that we may find to build relationships and position ourselves at the heart of our school's business. As Ross Todd has said, 'We need to focus on three things: connections, not collections; actions, not positions; and evidence, not advocacy' (Todd, 2001). Therefore, on the foundation of inspiration and the building of integration we now move the focus to innovation, because without it we cannot continue to evolve.

CHAPTER 9

Innovation

To innovate involves taking risks. Paradoxically this may happen most easily when people work in a safe and secure environment, one which encourages them to experiment in order to turn problems into opportunities. As librarians, many of us do not find ourselves in such a supportive situation, so why should we bother to invest energy, enthusiasm and hard work into something that might fail?

We may prefer to maintain the status quo rather than bring any extra stress on ourselves but, as we saw in Chapter 1, being professional involves looking continually for ways to improve our services. Just as a business cannot afford to stand still but needs to introduce new ideas and technologies to keep ahead of its competitors, so school librarians should not stagnate in the world of educational change and development. Furthermore, we all need intellectual stimulation to sustain our interest and innovating is a good way to keep us motivated and fresh.

Ross Todd (Todd, 2001) exhorts school librarians to re-conceptualize the role of the library, turning it from an information place into a knowledge-making space (see quotation at the end of Chapter 8). Using his three drivers for change: connections, actions and evidence, we will explore innovative practice for school librarians.

Connect

The pathways to innovation may open up to us through the contacts and relationships we make in our school, professional or wider communities. For instance, we may look at the leaders in our field and ask ourselves what is special about the librarians whom we admire. We can gain inspiration and insight from seeing how well they innovate and re-invent their roles (Taylor and Guiney, 2008); prizes for achievement such as the School Librarian of the Year Award in the UK help to draw attention to good practice (School Library Association, 2015b). It does not matter which model of professional practice we choose to follow as long as we continue to develop our ideas. The vignette below explains how it is possible to be innovative without necessarily being an extrovert.

At a meeting of local librarians there was discussion about raising profiles and professionalism, which evoked a lively debate. Sean told the group that he did not participate greatly in meetings at school, often leaving the discussion to others. When he had a new idea he would often use his blog to promote it rather than speaking directly to colleagues. This enabled him to refine, reflect and invite comment about the suggestion before putting it into practice. Although on the face of it Sean might not have appeared an innovative person, his skills as a listener and quiet practitioner, alongside his active use of social media to promote new ideas, contributed to his being held in high regard by his school and librarian communities.

So as we can see, innovation is not always about leading from the front – we can adopt an approach that suits our personality to achieve the same innovatory ends.

Often innovation comes from being 'inspired' by conversations with other librarians or reading about a new initiative and realizing that it could be applied to one's situation. It can also spring from a chance conversation with a teaching colleague. In these small-scale cases the new idea may just 'happen' and no formal planning takes place, as Richard's story shows.

Richard had worked as a librarian in a large state secondary school for three years and was aware that 'reading' was coming to the top of the agenda. In a conversation with an English Department colleague, he argued that narrative non-fiction could encourage reading. In a follow-up e-mail he quoted from influential articles to back his argument that biography, manga and graphic novels should be approved reading for pleasure in English classes. As a result of a discussion at the English Department meeting he was invited to hold 'reading surgeries' during English lessons to give personal advice and recommend titles to individuals.

Richard's approach demonstrates that innovation can require us to raise our heads above the parapet. The networks and connections we form within our communities enable us to take this risk and to act on our ideas. How can Richard now capitalize on this recognition of his contribution and act strategically?

Act

In Chapter 1 we discussed different models of professional discourse. These illustrate the importance of recognizing that we are not working in a static environment and show how we need to move with the times in order to gain respect and status. Some of us may feel uncomfortable with the idea of stepping over the safe boundaries of our day-to-day work, so is innovation important for everyone? The crucial factor is that we continue to evolve our role according to the dynamics of our working environment. This inevitably involves a degree of innovation, including introducing and trialling new ideas.

Continuing to develop our professional practice has long been recognized as a key feature of leadership (Roberts and Rowley, 2008). Having the confidence to implement our ideas is of utmost importance, and can be rewarding when we gain a sense of personal achievement. Innovation should not be seen as threatening but 'can and should be interesting and exciting' (Newton and Tarrant, 1992). Taking just small steps to introduce a new initiative can be very satisfying and may help to increase interest in the library and raise the status of the librarian and the library.

However, even if we are committed to innovation it can still seem very daunting to implement. Planning tools designed for managing change may help us take positive action and drive innovation forward, especially if some people are likely to disagree with our proposal.

A good way to begin is to consider these reflective questions:

- What do we want to do?
- Who will benefit?
- Who can we involve?
- How can we make it happen?
- Where will the time and resources come from?
- What difference will it make?

Other tools will become useful at different points in the process. A SWOT analysis is one such tool (see example in Appendix 4). Andrew successfully adopted a SWOT analysis to move his library forward.

Andrew was appointed to modernize the school library by amalgamating the two existing separate libraries and creating a learning resources centre for the whole school. He used the year between his arrival and the completed re-build to prove his usefulness and to earn the professional respect of the teachers by, for example, collaborating in teaching fiction lessons. As part of his campaign to put over his vision he completed a SWOT analysis, which he showed to key members of staff to demonstrate what he felt was wrong with the current situation and how the opportunity of the re-build could be used to great benefit, such as by developing a shared reading culture using the new learning resources centre. Not all staff shared his vision. In particular, some English teachers were accustomed to using the fiction library as a classroom for sustained silent reading. They could only see what they would lose with a library that they would have to share with other classes and individuals. In the end, though, Andrew went ahead, winning over a critical mass from within the English Department as his ideas were realized and they saw the new facilities in action.

Whole school policy making and planning procedures are also sometimes helpful for developing a new idea but they should be used with caution. They can have the opposite effect and simply maintain the status quo by inhibiting innovation rather than encouraging a critical, developmental eye. On the other hand, at its best, a planning conversation with a line manager can push us to stretch ourselves, be daring and achieve beyond our safety zone. In the vignette below, Frances shows how such a strategy can be implemented with a positive outcome.

Each year Frances produced an improvement plan, which she sent to her line manager and heard no more about. Then a new line manager was appointed and the school's planning procedures were made more rigorous.

At meeting with her line manager Frances presented her draft improvement plan and explained her hopes and difficulties. She found it empowering to have someone to exchange ideas with and in the course of the discussions she learned a lot about what was going on elsewhere in the school. For example, her target of working on the library VLE page was removed from the plan because the line manager advised that the school was concentrating on setting up a web based social media platform. Instead, a target relating to library involvement in talks and training about the social media replacement was introduced.

Frances also wanted to develop a whole school approach to information literacy; through talking about what was realistic and timely she and her line manager arrived at some objectives that were challenging, yet attainable. At least, the line manager saw no problem with three science teachers allowing Frances to run her pilot project in their lessons. Frances, on her own, would never have committed herself to something this specific in case others would think she was being presumptuous. What is more, she knew that when she proposed her ideas to more classes in subsequent years they would feature in the discussions of those classes as part of the next planning cycle.

Evidence

In Chapter 6 we discussed the crucial importance of using published evidence and generating our own. It is not enough to advocate new initiatives without providing supporting evidence; similarly we need to evaluate the benefit and value for students of implementing new ideas, technologies or designs. Most teachers have to provide statistical analysis from their lessons to show progression in their students' work. They can then use this information to amend their lesson plans if it shows that the students are not achieving targets or are finding some aspects of work less easy to understand than others. Using the evidence-based 'rolling evaluation' approach can also help a librarian to introduce innovative ideas successfully.

In this section on evidence we will focus on recognition of excellence, one type of evidence that we are successfully engaging in effective practices. In the first edition of this book we noted that innovation was recognized and celebrated through a number of awards given by school library organizations and other libraries worldwide. However those specific to school librarians seem to have fallen by the wayside in the last couple of years: The School Library Association of Victoria (2015) did not run an innovation award in 2013 though it has since been re-instated, while the International Association of School Librarianship did not accept nominations for this award in 2015 (International Association of School Librarianship, 2015).

Some current awards reward the library rather than the librarian. For example the SLA Inspiration Award (School Library Association, 2015a) is given for new library design but also considers the impact design has on creativity and engagement with learning. A review of past winners of CILIP's (2015) Libraries Change Lives Award shows that it is dominated by the public library service; school libraries have not won the award since 2007. Other awards still exist, but these are not specifically for school librarians.

The Florida Library Association's Library Innovation Award is designed 'to recognize a Florida library that has displayed innovative methods, projects, products, or organizational enhancements, such as using current and emerging technologies for library processes or information service delivery, but is not specific to School Libraries' (Florida Library Association, 2015).

It may be that the current state of the economy has contributed to sponsors withdrawing financial support from awards. Although it is disappointing to see the demise of and changes to these awards, what are the implications of this trend for innovation at school library level? Does it make it less likely to occur? We might argue that money has and always will be an issue, but still a way is found, and it is not the thought of an award that drives these changes in a school.

Despite this lack of recognition we still consider it is important to innovate, and this intrinsic belief might hold more value to us than a bestowed award. Even though it is an increasingly daunting prospect to introduce new ideas in a climate where it is deemed safer only to offer proven services, we need to be dynamic, if only because students' needs change. 'Think about where your students dwell: YouTube, MySpace, Facebook, mobile phones? Consider making a presence in these social networks to create conversations about your library and to stream information to your students' (Dickinson and Repman, 2015).

Of course, it is not only school library organizations that have recognized the importance of innovation. The Headmasters' and Headmistresses' Conference in the UK has published a series of case studies of innovation and good practice in leading independent schools. These include an example of a school library project on teaching information literacy skills and a case study of a school where the library acts as 'an information hub for the whole college community' and 'librarians manage the school website, intranet and extranet, coordinating the organization of content from the whole community' (Trafford, 2006). Recently, the All Party Parliamentary Group report *The Beating Heart of the School* (2014) describes how school libraries and librarians can make a direct impact on education and gives useful examples.

Managing change

We have found that when planning to innovate there are a number of things to consider:

- the scope of the innovation
- the nature of the organization
- key factors in implementing change
- how to prioritize activities
- how to work with people.

The scope of the innovation

Clarity about these elements is vital when considering the scope of an innovation:

- How big is the change that you are trying to introduce?
- What range of activities is needed in order to make it successful?
- Who needs to be involved?

The nature of the organization

It is important to understand how the school works and how ready it is to engage with change. This will help to ensure that the processes used and steps taken to bring about change fit comfortably with the way the school operates. If we manage change in a way that is not congruent with the environment it will at best produce more conflict than necessary and at worst not produce the results that we want, as we discussed in Chapter 5. (See Appendix 5 for a discussion of how to choose priorities when development planning.) Innovation involves many different activities; the paths to achieving the same result look different in different schools.

Key factors in implementing a change

It is important to make a systematic analysis of the factors in school that will support the innovation and those that might hinder it. Carrying out a force field analysis (Mind Tools, 2015) can help to weigh the pros and cons of a situation; this enables us to draw up a sensible action plan based on our real environments. An example of how force field analysis can be used is presented in Appendix 6.

How to prioritize activities

Managing any change involves us in choosing priorities. What should we work on in order to support the process of change as effectively as possible? None of us have unlimited time, energy or resources, so we need to focus activity on what we think will be most productive in our environment. What do we really need to pay attention to as a matter of priority? When everything appears to be important people can be reluctant to prioritize. However, studies of change have shown that success is more likely when a clear focus is sustained on a limited number of factors.

How to work with people

Working with people is probably the most challenging part of managing change. We need to think hard about what we want people to do differently, how to present it to them and how to support them in changing. We also need to be clear about the effect that the innovation will have on our roles and activities.

Process and principles of managing change

Although the People's Network Change Management Toolkit (Information Management Associates, 2004) is rather dated, it still offers a convenient round-up of the core processes and principles of managing change in libraries. The Toolkit reminds us that 'significant innovation will take time' and that most significant change processes are likely to take at least three years. It outlines the process of change and the different activities needed at each stage. See Appendix 7 for an outline of these steps, which are based on the work of Michael Fullan (2007).

The Toolkit also spells out some important principles about monitoring the progress of an innovation, finding supporters and allies, having a clear vision, choosing something that will have early impact, communicating progress and success to other people, and realizing that not everyone will be prepared to change. All these principles must be taken into consideration if the development is to be successful (see Appendix 7).

Using whole school processes and the key change agents

In Chapter 5 we said that it is important to offer solutions to senior management rather than to air our complaints or problems. The same holds true when we attempt to innovate or manage change. This vignette shows how change can be introduced successfully by presenting a positive initiative.

Few pupils at Linda's school borrowed reading books from their school library; school librarian Linda was due to meet her line manager to discuss this. She had read that the subject of supporting students with special educational needs was becoming a high priority in many schools, and many of these students qualified for Pupil Premium funding. She knew that this would be a golden opportunity to show what she could do. Using the UK school librarians' self-evaluation document (Markless and Streatfield, 2004), she prepared a list of possible action points, and checked them with a senior teaching colleague. She then included her action list in a memo to the special educational needs co-ordinator (SENCO) in charge of the initiative. Her colleague welcomed her unsolicited contribution as supportive and positive and followed up on every one of the ideas Linda had suggested. Linda was invited to be part of the working group to take things forward and her line manager was impressed that rather than complaining about lack of use of the library Linda had strong proposals to bring about change.

By linking her ideas to a whole school initiative and submitting them to a senior teacher, Linda has successfully matched her action points to a perceived need in the school and found a supporter and advocate for her cause. These are two of the essential steps identified by Michael Fullan (2007) in the first phase of implementing change.

However, the following assumptions must also be made:

- Conflict and disagreement are not only inevitable but fundamental.
- No amount of knowledge will make it totally clear what action should be taken.
- Change is a frustrating, discouraging business so expect and plan for setbacks. Don't be discouraged when they happen; it would be more surprising if they didn't   (Fullan, 2007).

The next vignette shows that even when we are confident in our role and feel reasonably safe in proposing a new initiative, we can be discouraged and encounter setbacks.

School librarian Barbara had established herself as a respected member of staff at her state secondary school so when she offered to attend Year 7 and 8 parent–teacher consultation evenings to give advice to parents on how to support their children's reading, the English teachers were very keen on the idea (even if some were a little puzzled that she should have 'volunteered' for extra evening work). Librarians from other schools who heard about the innovation were very impressed and one even went on to volunteer to do the same in the school where she worked. However, even though Barbara could hear her teaching colleagues recommending that parents speak to her, Year 7 parents seemed to be nervous, overwhelmed by the consultation evening, and fixed on seeing every teacher; they could not spare the time to speak to Barbara. Year 8 parents were more open to the suggestion, and 19 of them consulted Barbara during the three-hour period, but the others ignored the teachers' prompting. The limited take-up was very disappointing because Barbara had felt that the idea was a huge leap forward.

Barbara will need to consider whether in future years her presence will become more accepted and maybe even expected, or whether she could spend the time more usefully on other things, because 'effective change or innovation takes time' (Hargreaves and Hopkins, 1994). Meanwhile, she was fortunate that her spirits were sustained by the fact that the English teachers had so readily taken up her idea, demonstrating their trust and respect.

Innovation inevitably involves change, both organizational and personal, which by its nature can be problematic; we may meet with resistance from other members of our school community. We can manage change successfully if we understand the various processes involved.

Innovation is difficult and uncomfortable and requires courage and determination, but can be exciting and reaffirm why we continue to be school librarians. It is challenging but necessary to maintain inspiration and integration. Being innovative is at the heart of thinking and acting strategically.

We wrote this book with the aim of prompting school librarians to stand back from their day-to-day activity and critically re-examine their values, philosophy and what defines their professional practice. It is for this reason that this final chapter concerns innovation, which with all its risks and challenges demonstrates the best way that we can renew our professional identity.

APPENDIX 1

Levels of education

Table A1.1 shows the levels of education, mediators for and examples of each set out by Kuhlthau (1993).

Table A1.1 Levels of education		
Level	Role	Descriptor
1	Organizer	No instruction: • self-service search in an organized collection.
2	Lecturer	Orienteering instruction: • single session • overview of services, policies and location of facility and collection • no specific problem.
3	Instructor	Single-source instruction: • variety of independent sessions • instruction on one type of source to address specific problems.
4	Tutor	Strategy instruction: • series of sessions • instruction on sequence of sources to address specific problem.
5	Counsellor	Process instruction: • holistic interaction over time • instruction on identifying and interpreting information to address evolving problem.

Source: Kuhlthau (1993)

APPENDIX 2

School library self-evaluation questions

Table A2.1 School library self-evaluation questions

Key library self-evaluation questions	Secondary school self-evaluation form questions	Evidence examples
1 How high are standards?	3a How well do learners achieve, and how high are their standards?	• Assessment of learning of students in library-based work • Examples of work produced
2 How well are pupils' attitudes, values and personal qualities developed?	4 How good is the overall personal development and well-being of the learners?	• Evidence of consultation with students • Range of supportive materials • Overall atmosphere in the library
3 How effective are teaching and learning?	5a How good is the quality of teaching and learning?	• External viewpoints – local authority audits, Ofsted, HM Inspectorate • Internal lesson observations • Visiting librarians (can help to establish the library as a good model in eyes of external and therefore of internal eyes) • Assessment of learning of students in library-based work
4 How well does library provision meet pupils' needs?	5b How well do the curriculum and other activities meet the range of needs and interests of learners?	• Feedback from students, parents and teachers • Record of resources used in research work
5 How well are pupils guided and supported?	5c How well are learners guided and supported?	• Assessment data on student reading and writing • Homework club reports to tutors to highlight regular attenders and observation of their needs • Library displays and website material

Key library self-evaluation questions	Secondary school self-evaluation form questions	Evidence examples
6 How effectively does the library work with parents and the community?	2 What are the views of learners, parents or carers and other stakeholders, including hard to reach groups, and how do you know?	• Parent voice via survey tool • Letters to home about homework club and reading achievements • Library newsletter
7 How well is the learning resource centre (LRC) or library led and managed?	6a What is the overall effectiveness of leadership and management?	• Line management review • Annual report • Stakeholders' voices via survey tool

Based on: Markless and Streatfield (2004)

An example of a completed self-evaluation summary sheet

We recognize that many school librarians are required to use their school's in-house documentation for self-evaluation, but felt we should include this example of a completed self-evaluation summary sheet (Figure A3.1) from Markless and Streatfield (2004) as it was still useful.

Summary Sheet for Key Question 3: *How effective are teaching and learning?* and Strand 3b: *Co-operation between LRC staff and teaching staff to ensure effective learning*

What is your reason for your choice of key question and strand?
We work very well with some curriculum areas but there are a number of departments that use the library as a room without drawing on the librarian's support and expertise in any way.

Indicator	Level awarded in last evaluation	Evidence collected	Level self awarded (1–5)	What should the LRC do to improve?
1 Do Learning Resource Centre (LRC) staff and teachers plan and teach collaboratively for LRC-based lessons and courses?	n/a	Diary showing lessons taught collaboratively Worksheets	3	Work on formalizing collaborative teaching by preparing formal lesson plans for lessons
2 Do LRC and teaching staff collaborate to ensure that research and study skills are taught and assessed in appropriate places throughout the curriculum?	n/a	Record of recent work as research mentor for individual A-level students in History and Media Studies Lesson taught to A level Geography & A level Science Discussions with Science teachers about 'Science in the News' project. Induction programme for Year 7	2	Map information literacy skills delivery in the library across the years and use the process to raise discussion with teachers; (references in schemes of work would be a more long-term whole school issue)

Indicator	Level awarded in last evaluation	Evidence collected	Level self awarded (1–5)	What should the LRC do to improve?
3 Do departments include effective LRC use in their schemes of work and homework tasks?	n/a	Annual reports to individual subject departments	4	Analyse homework tasks for indications of LRC use
4 Do LRC staff work in partnership with the SENCO, gifted and talented co-ordinator and English as an additional language co-ordinator?	n/a	Reports to SENCO and gifted and talented co-ordinator	3	
5 Are teachers involved in the selection of LRC resources and in the development of the LRC and its role within the school?	n/a	Examples of teachers' written requests for stock and minutes of meetings with individual heads of dept		Step up reporting to departments so that it becomes an annual review
6 Is there an effective induction programme to the LRC for all staff new to the school?	n/a	Librarian takes part in the induction programme for new staff – 15 minute talk Outline of library use in staff handbook	3	Interview last year's new teachers using document 'Questions for Staff'
7 Do LRC staff lead INSET and provide informal training for teaching staff?	n/a	Examples of ad hoc training and informal discussions (No formal INSET)	3	
Support required to enable the LRC to improve: Advice from line manager on lesson planning				
Overall level reached: 3				

Figure A3.1 Example of a completed self-evaluation summary sheet

Original grid: Markless and Streatfield (2004)

APPENDIX 4

SWOT analysis

A SWOT analysis is a strategic planning tool that helps us to assess overall feasibility of a new initiative, service or activity. We can use this tool to analyse systematically the strengths and weaknesses on which the success of any new initiative will depend, the opportunities that exist for its development and the potential threats to its success (Figure A4.1). It is useful to carry out a SWOT analysis when considering a new initiative, for example a new online service or whether to adopt a different information literacy approach.

Strengths, e.g. advantages; knowledge; capabilities; resources; experience; likely benefits; value; cultural, behavioural and attitudinal aspects	**Weaknesses**, e.g. disadvantages, gaps in capabilities or knowledge; timescale; workload pressures; effect on core activities; resources; reliability of plan; predictability of outcome; level of support
Opportunities, e.g. organizational trends; educational agenda; new partnerships; technology development; seasonal, fashion or cultural influences	**Threats**, e.g. political effects; de-stabilization of core activities or sustainable finance; loss of key partners; IT developments; competing services or activities

Figure A4.1 The different elements of a SWOT analysis

An example of a SWOT analysis

Meena worked as a librarian at a large school. Generally the library was well used but she had noticed that some departments, particularly the Maths Department, rarely used the facilities. She had recently read an article in the School Library Service newsletter about another school librarian in her area who had been successful in encouraging classes into libraries to do number puzzles. Meena decided to make a SWOT analysis to explore whether this would work within her context (Figure A4.2).

Strengths	**Weaknesses**
• Article shows other schools have used this successfully • Library well stocked with puzzle books • Number puzzles popular generally	• May lack sufficient mathematical expertise to assist students during the class • Will have less time for cataloguing, etc. and could create a workload pressure
Opportunities	**Threats**
• The Maths Department will be demonstrating a commitment to the literacy agenda by promoting library visits • Will help students' numerical abilities • Will make a clear link between the library improvement plan and the school improvement plan goals • Will help pupils become comfortable with the library environment in a different subject • Could lead to more projects	• Maths Department staff may say they are too busy with curriculum • Other departments that are high users may get upset if they cannot book as much time because the Maths Department students are due to use the space

Figure A4.2 Example of a SWOT analysis

Meena decided that she had enough strengths and opportunities information to make a strong case to the Maths Department to carry out an experimental lesson.

APPENDIX 5

Choosing priorities in development planning: sample grid

One source (Hargreaves and Hopkins, 1994) suggests that in order to draw up a development plan that is likely to be effective, we need to choose our activities carefully. One way of doing this is to create a grid and list down one side all the activities we would like, or have, to undertake over the next year. Across the top of the grid we identify whether these activities are unavoidable, urgent, desirable, large in size and scope, small in size and scope, and have strong roots (already part of the school's established practice), weak roots, strong links to priorities and weak links to priorities. Figure A5.1 shows an example of a grid used when choosing priorities for a school improvement plan.

Activity	Unavoidable	Urgent	Desirable	Large in size and scope	Small in size and scope	Strong roots	Weak roots	Strong links to priorities	Weak links to priorities
Year 9 reading challenge	✓			✓		✓		✓	
Guitar-building workshop			✓		✓		✓	✓	
Poetry jam sessions at lunchtime			✓		✓		✓	✓	
Extra reading assessment in autumn term for Year 7	✓	✓	✓	✓		✓		✓	
Library assistant training			✓		✓	✓		✓	

Figure A5.1 Example of a grid used when choosing priorities for a school improvement plan

This approach provides a basis on which to choose our priorities, as any plan needs to include a balanced group of items to make it manageable. Some things must be done, some are personally rewarding and therefore highly motivating, and some are speculative in nature but have the potential to yield a powerful or interesting impact. Not all our proposed activities would contribute towards the school targets and therefore may not have strong roots and links.

Once we have listed all of the activities, we need to be pragmatic when selecting those to include on our improvement plan. School goals must be achieved but can they also be satisfied by undertaking projects that are personally rewarding? Being committed to many initiatives that have strong roots or links could lead to sizeable work pressures and little reward. What does it take to keep us motivated and engaged?

Adapted from: Hargreaves and Hopkins (1994)

APPENDIX 6

Example of a force field analysis: a tool for managing change

A force field analysis is a useful tool to help us analyse the forces that will support any change we wish to make and the forces that will reduce the chance of its success. We first need to identify as many factors as possible that will influence the proposed change. Then we assign a score to each factor, e.g. 2 = weak and 5 = strong. When totalled we can then make an informed decision. Figure A6.1 shows an example of a force field analysis, carried out when considering whether to develop the library's role within the new Steps curriculum (Hornsby, 2014).[1]

---

[1] In 2013 in the UK it was announced that central government was no longer going to dictate how schools should record and report pupil progress between statutory tests. Levels within the curriculum to which teaching and assessment had been tied were removed. Schools began looking at new ways of supporting and tracking pupil progress, generating evidence on which to make decisions about the next steps in instruction. This has involved consideration of providing a richer variety of tasks, the development of tools such as 'learning ladders' to make progress more visible, engaging pupils in self-assessment and planning their next steps, and using new technological tools to track pupils' progress. This 'culture change' has implications for the library's engagement in setting up opportunities for pupils to demonstrate learning and for capturing pupil's achievements and progress.

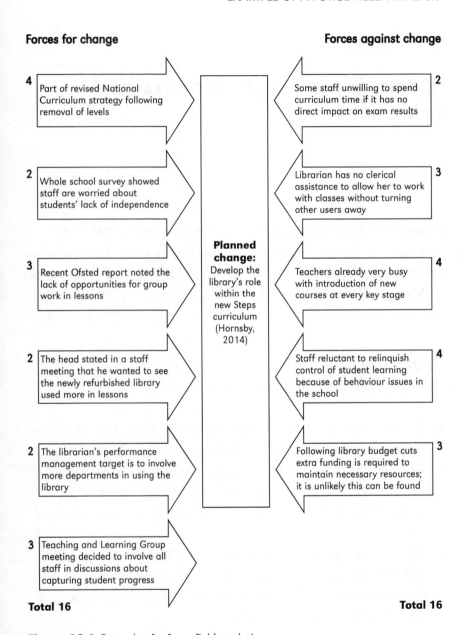

Forces for change

4 | Part of revised National Curriculum strategy following removal of levels

2 | Whole school survey showed staff are worried about students' lack of independence

3 | Recent Ofsted report noted the lack of opportunities for group work in lessons

2 | The head stated in a staff meeting that he wanted to see the newly refurbished library used more in lessons

2 | The librarian's performance management target is to involve more departments in using the library

3 | Teaching and Learning Group meeting decided to involve all staff in discussions about capturing student progress

Total 16

Planned change: Develop the library's role within the new Steps curriculum (Hornsby, 2014)

Forces against change

Some staff unwilling to spend curriculum time if it has no direct impact on exam results | 2

Librarian has no clerical assistance to allow her to work with classes without turning other users away | 3

Teachers already very busy with introduction of new courses at every key stage | 4

Staff reluctant to relinquish control of student learning because of behaviour issues in the school | 4

Following library budget cuts extra funding is required to maintain necessary resources; it is unlikely this can be found | 3

Total 16

Figure A6.1 Example of a force field analysis

Managing change: process and principles

Phases of implementation in the change process

Librarians need to pay attention to various factors in the change process when trying to innovate. The steps set out below, based on the work of Michael Fullan (2007), are not a blueprint or programme for managing change as the elements are different in different locations.

Stage 1 Initiation

Tie change into perceived needs and priorities:

- Find a strong advocate to talk to those likely to be affected and get concrete support from influential people in the school.
- Consult widely. At this stage it is not usually a good idea to try to involve everyone. However, those likely to be affected need to be kept informed of what is happening, what is being considered, and so on.
- Develop clear processes to engage people with the change and to make developments as transparent as possible (e.g. using checklists, exercises for students). Everyone needs a good idea of what they should be doing differently.

At this stage the focus is on the innovation: what is it all about? What are the implications? How important and relevant is it?

Stage 2 Implementation

At the implementation stage the main focus is on people: helping and encouraging colleagues to adopt the innovation:

- All change needs a co-ordinator to keep things moving and to orchestrate the process. Co-ordinators need to be sensitive and flexible.
- Local empowerment must be supported by enabling staff other than managers to take some control over the process. Perhaps they can be involved in deciding priorities or what to do first. Some local adaptation should be encouraged. Teachers always want to adapt an innovation to their teaching approach.
- Be ready with advice, technical assistance and troubleshooting, vital components of any implementation. Too often such support is readily available near the beginning of any innovation but fizzles out when people really need help.
- Tangible benefits and rewards of the innovation need to be made apparent (early concrete practices). Show what the innovation can do to meet a perceived need in the school. Are more students engaging with a subject? Are more boys reading? Publicize examples of success. People are more likely to be persuaded by seeing the benefits than by being told how good an innovation is or will be.

Stage 3 Incorporation

At the incorporation stage consider the following points:

- Make sure that the innovation has been built into institutional mechanisms and systems, and the way in which the institution functions (e.g. staff development; budgeting, curriculum development and assessment), or the committee structure may need to be changed.

- Competing demands from new initiatives, policies and government requirements may cause attention and resources to be switched away from what we are trying to achieve. How can the time, energy and resources needed to continue this work be protected in the face of competing demands? Does something else need to be thrown out or demoted to prevent too many conflicting demands being made on staff? Who is in a position to sort out these priorities?
- Induction for new staff at all levels must incorporate the innovation.
- Build up a critical mass of users. This will help keep up momentum and show how important it is to sustain the change. However, do not expect everyone to adopt an innovation.

At this stage the main focus is on the organization and how it functions. Can it adapt its systems and procedures to accommodate the new demands? Or will it merely try to bolt this innovation on to an existing bureaucracy, so the change is unlikely to stick in the long term?

Those trying to innovate need to understand how the change process occurs but they also need to keep some general principles in mind. These are helpful when things are not proceeding as hoped or when we get impatient at the often slow rate of progress.

Key principles of managing change

These are the key principles of managing change:

- Monitor the progress of the innovation carefully. Be prepared to step in and slow things down or change direction if the innovating is moving too quickly or is not having the desired impact (not a good return on the investment of time and effort).
- Build alliances: network to find supporters and advocates. We cannot do it by ourselves.
- Think big: we all need a clear vision of what success looks like and are sustained by what we might achieve – the overall aims of the innovation. But act small: plan for steady progress and take measured steps towards implementing the vision.
- Avoid 'brute sanity': It is tempting when trying to promote change to give lots of clear, loud messages to staff about how wonderful the innovation is, how it will revolutionize student learning, reading and motivation and so on. This is brute sanity. And if the messages are said often and loudly enough, staff will tend to back off and build barriers to hide behind! Missionaries tend to make poor change agents. People need space to work out their position and decide how to deal with the innovation.
- Get some early concrete practices in place: Choose something that will have some impact fairly quickly but don't worry if it is not perfect. An early showcase of what is possible will help persuade and build alliances.
- Keep people informed about progress, successes, impact; publicize your services; show benefits in practice.
- Be prepared to work very hard.
- Do not expect all or even most to change: one useful reminder of what to expect when proposing worthwhile change is the adage that 30% of people will be prepared to support and participate in it; 40% will keep their distance and need to be persuaded with good evidence that the innovation meets a real need and is worth

the investment of their time and energy – they can be won over; 30% will not change.

Use these principles as a package. You cannot just choose the ones that you like if you want change to be effective.

Adapted from: Fullan (2007)

References

American Association of School Librarians (2007) *Standards for the 21st Century Learner*, Chicago IL, www.ala.org/aasl/standards-guidelines/learning-standards (accessed 12 December 2015).

Atherton, J. S. (2013) *Learning and Teaching; Cognitive Dissonance and Learning*, www.learningandteaching.info/learning/dissonance.htm (accessed 15 November 2015).

Barrett, L. and Douglas, J. (2004) *CILIP Guidelines for Secondary School Libraries*, 2nd edn, London, Facet Publishing.

BBC (2014) *GCSE Bitesize: business studies: setting objectives*, www.bbc.co.uk/schools/gcsebitesize/business/aims/partnershiprev2.shtml (accessed 29 November 2015).

Birdwell, J. and Bani, M. (2014) *Introducing Generation Citizen*, London, Demos, www.demos.co.uk/files/Generation_Citizen_-_web.pdf?1392764120 (accessed 12 December 2015).

Bishop, J. L. (2013) *The Flipped Classroom: a survey of the research*, www.studiesuccesho.nl/wp-content/uploads/2014/04/flipped-classroom-artikel.pdf (accessed 12 December 2015).

Bloom, B. S. (ed.) (1956) *Taxonomy of Educational Objectives: the classification of educational goals. Handbook I: the cognitive domain*, New York, David McKay.

Brophy, P., Craven, J. and Markland M. (2008) *Libraries Without Walls 7: exploring 'anywhere, anytime'*, London, Facet Publishing.

California Department for Education (2011) *Model School Library Standards for California Public Schools: kindergarten through grade twelve*, Sacramento CA, California Department for Education.

Chartered Institute of Library and Information Professionals (2014a) *New Framework of Professional Registration*, www.cilip.org.uk/cilip/advocacy-awards-and-projects/projects-and-reviews/future-skills-project/new-framework (accessed 26 November 2015).

Chartered Institute of Library and Information Professionals (2014b) *CILIP Salary Guidelines for School Librarians 2014–15*, www.cilip.org.uk/sites/default/files/documents/CILIP%20School%20Librarian%20Salary%20Guidelines%202014-15.pdf (accessed 30 November 2015).

Chartered Institute of Library and Information Professionals (2015) 'CILIP Libraries Change Lives Award', www.cilip.org.uk/cilip/cilip-libraries-change-lives-award (accessed 2 December 2015).

Chartered Institute of Library and Information Professionals, School Libraries Group (2013) *Professional Librarians: leaflet*, www.cilip.org.uk/school-libraries-group/professional-librarians-leaflet (accessed 8 December 2015).

Chartered Institute of Library and Information Professionals in Scotland (2014) *School Librarianship: an advocacy strategy*, http://static1.1.sqspcdn.com/static/f/825826/25593957/1422010188403/advocacystrategy.pdf?token=%2FNrpkvOMNgLJXHL3rPZZmak%2FFI1E%3D (accessed 6 December 2015).

Christie, J. (2008) Stand up for the Brand 'Libraries = Books = Reading', *CILIP Update*, **7** (5), May, 26.

Coates, T. (2013) *The Ideal Library*, blog, Huffpost Books, 16 March, www.huffingtonpost.com/tim-coates/the-ideal-library_b_2459140.html (accessed 26 November 2015).

Cohen, L., Manion, L. and Morrison, K. (2007) *Research Methods in Education*, 6th edn, London, Routledge.

Day, E., Kington, A., Stobart, G. and Sammons P. (2006) The Personal and Professional Selves of Teachers: stable and unstable identities, *British Educational Research Journal*, **32** (4), 601–16.

Department for Children, Schools and Families (2008) *Knight: extended projects will help prepare students for work and university*, press notice 2008/0173, London, 14 August.

Department for Education (2014a) *The Equality Act 2010 and Schools: departmental advice for school leaders, school staff, governing bodies and local authorities*, https://www.gov.uk/government/uploads/system/ uploads/attachment_data/file/315587/Equality_Act_Advice_Final.pdf (accessed 23 January 2016).

Department for Education (2014b) *Statutory Guidance: National Curriculum in England: framework for key stages 1 to 4*, https://www.gov.uk/government/ publications/national-curriculum-in-england-framework-for-key- stages-1-to-4 (accessed 16 December 2015).

Devonshire, I. M., Davis, J., Fairweather, S., Highfield, L., Thaker, C., Walsh, A., Wilson, R. and Hathway, G. J. (2014) *Risk-Based Learning Games Improve Long-Term Retention of Information among School Pupils*, http://journals.plos.org/plosone/article?id=10.1371/journal.pone. 0103640#pone-0103640-g004 (accessed 29 November 2015).

Dickinson, G. and Repman, J. (2015) *School Library Management*, 7th edn, Santa Barbara, California, ABC-CLIO.

Festinger, L. (1957) *A Theory of Cognitive Dissonance*, Stanford CA, Stanford University Press.

Fielding, M. and Bragg, S. (2003) *Students as Researchers: making a difference*, Cambridge, Pearson.

Fish, D. and De Cossart, L. (2006) Thinking Outside The (Tick) Box: rescuing professionalism and professional judgement, *Medical Education*, **40** (5), 403–4.

Florida Library Association (2015) Library Innovation Award, www.flalib.org/awards_descriptions/Library%20Innovation%20Award.pdf

(accessed 2 December 2015).

Forsyth, D. R. (2006) *Group Dynamics*, 4th edn, Belmont CA, Thomson Wadsworth.

Foucault, M. (1972) *The Archaeology of Knowledge*, London, Tavistock.

Fullan, M. G. (2007) *The New Meaning of Educational Change*, 4th edn, London, Routledge.

Gilham, B. (2005) *Research Interviewing: the range of techniques: a practical guide*, Milton Keynes, Open University Press.

Gravells, A. (2014) *The Award in Education and Training*, London, Sage.

Hargreaves, A. (2000) *Changing Teachers, Changing Times: teachers' work and culture in the postmodern age*, London, Continuum International.

Hargreaves, D. H. and Hopkins, D. (1994) *Development Planning for School Improvement*, London, Cassell.

Hornsby, J. (2014) *The Road Beyond Levels*, https://prezi.com/01x5iqc9tujq/the-road-beyond-levels/ (accessed 3 January 2016).

Information Management Associates (2004) People's Network Change Management Toolkit, London, Museums, Libraries and Archives Council, http://trove.nla.gov.au/work/153629755?versionId=167512819; adaptation by Lambeth at www.sateo.co.uk/wp-content/uploads/2012/10/change-management-toolkit.pdf (accessed 20 December 2015).

International Association of School Librarianship (2015) IASL Grants and Awards, www.iasl-online.org/awards/index.html (accessed 2 December 2015).

International Federation of Library Associations (2006) *IFLA/UNESCO School Libraries Manifesto: the school library in teaching and learning for all*, www.ifla.org/publications/iflaunesco-school-library-manifesto-1999 (accessed 12 December 2015).

Invensis (2011) *Setting SMART Objectives*, www.bbc.co.uk/schools/gcsebitesize/business/aims/partnershiprev2.shtml (accessed 29 November 2015).

Kachel, D. E. (2013) *School Library Research Summarized*, Mansfield PA,

School Library & Information Technologies Department, Mansfield
University, http://sl-it.mansfield.edu/upload/MU-LibAdvoBklt2013.pdf
(accessed 12 December 2015).

Kuhlthau, C. C. (1993) *Seeking Meaning: a process approach to library and
information services*, Norwood NJ, Ablex.

Lance, K. C., Rodney, M. J. and Hamilton-Pennell, C. (2000) *How School
Librarians Help Kids Achieve Standards: the Second Colorado Study*,
Colorado, Library Research Service Colorado State Library,
www.lrs.org/documents/lmcstudies/CO/execsumm.pdf (accessed
12 December 2015).

Lankes, R. D. (2009) *Bullet Point: we live in Shakespearian times*,
http://quartz.syr.edu/blog/?p=692 (accessed 7 December 2015).

Lemaire, K. and Duncan, S. (2014) *Everything in its Place: managing electronic
and physical resources in the school library*, Swindon, School Library
Association.

Levy, T. W. (2013) *The Engagement Project: connecting with your consumer in the
participation age*, https://www.thinkwithgoogle.com/articles/engagement-
project-new-normal.html (accessed 12 December 2015).

Libraries All Party Parliamentary Group (2014) *The Beating Heart of the
School: improving educational attainment through school libraries and librarians*,
www.cilip.org.uk/sites/default/files/documents/BeatingHeartoftheSchool.
pdf (accessed 2 December 2015).

Loertscher, D. V. (2013) Makerspaces in the school library learning
commons and the uTEC maker model, *Teacher Librarian*, **41** (2), 48.

Markless, S. and Streatfield, D. (2004) *Improve Your Library: a self-evaluation
process for secondary school libraries and learning resource centres* 2 vols,
London, Department for Education and Skills, out of print, available at
www.informat.org/schoollibraries/primarynewuser.html and
www.informat.org/schoollibraries/secondarynewuser.html (accessed
20 December 2015).

Markless, S. and Streatfield, D. (2013) *Evaluating the Impact of Your Library*,

2nd edn, London, Facet Publishing.

Maslow, A. H. (1998) *Towards a Psychology of Being*, 3rd edn, London, Wiley.

Mind Tools Ltd (2015) *Force Field Analysis: analyzing the pressures for and against change,* www.mindtools.com/pages/article/newTED_06.htm (accessed 2 December 2015).

Morris, E. (chair) (2010) *School Libraries: a plan for improvement*, School Library Commission, Museums, Libraries & Archives Council and National Literacy Trust, www.literacytrust.org.uk/assets/0000/5718/School_Libraries_A_Plan_for_Improvement.pdf (accessed 23 January 2016).

Newton, C. and Tarrant, T. (1992) *Managing Change in Schools*, London, Routledge.

Nottingham Trent University (2013) *CADQ Guide: the flipped classroom*, Nottingham, Centre for Academic Development and Quality, Nottingham Trent University, https://www.ntu.ac.uk/adq/document_uploads/teaching/154084.pdf (accessed 12 December 2015).

Oberg, D. and Schultz-Jones, B. (eds) (2015) *IFLA School Library Guidelines*, 2nd edn, draft, School Libraries Standing Committee, International Federation of Library Associations, www.ifla.org/publications/node/9512 (accessed 12 December 2015).

Ofsted (2006) *Good School Libraries: making a difference to learning*, London, Ofsted.

Ofsted (2014) *Giving Pupils with Special Educational Needs a Voice*, https://www.gov.uk/government/publications/giving-pupils-with-special-educational-needs-a-voice (accessed 26 November 2015).

Oncken, W. Jr and Wass, D. L. (1999) Management Time: who's got the monkey?, *Harvard Business Review*, Nov–Dec, 1–8, https://hbr.org/1999/11/management-time-whos-got-the-monkey (accessed 15 November 2015).

Paquet, J. N. (2014) *Op-Ed: get the old grumpy librarians out; for our children's sake!*, www.digitaljournal.com/news/politics/op-ed-get-the-old-grumpy-librarians-out-for-our-children-s-sake/article/396092 (accessed 7 December 2015).

Reynolds, G. (2008) *Presentation Zen: inspiration matters*, www.presentationzen.com/presentationzen/2008/02/if-your-present.html (accessed 9 December 2015).

Roberts, N. (2014) *National Curriculum Review*, http://researchbriefings.files.parliament.uk/documents/SN06798/SN06798.pdf (accessed 12 December 2015).

Roberts, S. and Rowley, J. (2008) *Leadership: the challenge for the information profession*, London, Facet Publishing.

Rogers, J. and Frost, B. (2006) *Every Child Matters: empowering the student voice*, London, Department for Education and Skills.

Schmich, M. (2008) *Wear Sunscreen: a primer for real life*, Kansas City, Missouri, Andrews McMeel.

Scholastic Research Foundation (2008) *School libraries work!, research foundation paper*, 3rd edn, Danbury CT, Scholastic Library Publishing, www2.scholastic.com/content/collateral_resources/pdf/s/slw3_2008.pdf (accessed 9 December 2015).

Schon, D. (1983) *The Reflective Practitioner: how professionals think in action*, London, Temple Smith.

School Library Association (2011) *SLA Standards for Secondary School Libraries*, Swindon, School Library Association.

School Library Association (2015a) SLA Inspiration Award, www.sla.org.uk/inspiration-award.php (accessed 2 December 2015).

School Library Association (2015b) School Librarian of the Year Award 2015, www.sla.org.uk/slya-2015.php (accessed 2 December 2015).

School Library Association of Victoria (2015) Awards, http://slav.org.au/about-us/awards/ (accessed 2 December 2015).

Shaper, S. (ed.) (2014) *CILIP Guidelines for Secondary School Libraries*, 3rd edn, London, Facet Publishing.

Shaper, S. and Streatfield, D. (2012) Invisible care? The role of librarians in caring for the 'whole pupil' in secondary schools, *Pastoral Care in Education* **30** (1), 65–75.

Small, R. V. et al. (2007) *New York State's School Libraries and Media Specialists: an impact study*, Syracuse NY, Center for Digital Literacy, Syracuse University.

Stenhouse, L. (1975) *An Introduction to Curriculum Research and Development*, London, Heinemann.

Streatfield, D. and Markless, S. (1994) *Invisible Learning? The contribution of school libraries to teaching and learning*, Library and Information Research Report 98, London, British Library Research and Development Department.

Streatfield, D., Shaper, S. and Rae-Scott, S. (2010) *School Libraries in the UK: a worthwhile past, a difficult present – and a transformed future?*, main report of the UK National Survey, www.cilip.org.uk/sites/default/files/documents/full-school-libraries-report_0.pdf (accessed 16 December 2015).

Taylor, L. and Guiney, P. (2008) Leading the Way to Excellence, *Library and Information Gazette*, **25** July–7 August, 27.

Think Newsletter (2013) *Meet the YouTube generation*, www.thinkwithgoogle.com/articles/meet-gen-c-youtube-generation-in-own-words.html (accessed 12 December 2015).

Todd, R. J. (2001) Transitions for Preferred Futures of School Libraries: knowledge space, not information place; connections, not collections; actions, not positions; evidence, not advocacy, keynote address at 'Inspiring Connections: learning, libraries and literacies', the 30th conference of the International Association of School Librarianship, Waipuna Hotel, Auckland, 9–12 July.

Todd, R. J. (2005a) Information Literacy and Enquiry Learning: the role of the library, keynote lecture at 'Knowledge is Power: creating the information literate school', School Library Association Conference,

University of Surrey, Guildford, 17–19 June.

Todd, R. J. (2005b) School Libraries, Productive Pedagogy and Leading of Learning, presentation at School Library Association of Victoria Conference, www.slav.schools.net.au/downloads/08pastpapers/ 15learners/RToddAug2005.ppt

Todd, R. J. (2012) School Libraries as Pedagogical Centers, *Scan*, **31**, 27–36, http://scan.nsw.edu.au/ (accessed 12 December 2015).

Trafford, B. (ed.) (2006) *i² = Independent + Innovative: examples of innovation in HMC schools*, London, John Catt Educational Ltd.

Tripp, D. (1993) *Critical Incidents in Teaching: developing professional judgement*, London, Routledge.

Valenza, J. (2010) *Standards for 21st Century School Librarians*, Baexem, Netherlands, ENSIL Foundation.

Webb, C. (2012) Librarians are Leaders of Learning: leadership and the school library, *The School Librarian*, **60** (4), 201–3.

Webb, C. (2013) *Information Literacy and the Secondary School,* EdD thesis, Canterbury, Christ Church University, http://create.canterbury.ac.uk/ 13100/1/13100.pdf (accessed 9 December 2015).

Wellcome Trust (2011) Perspectives on Education: inquiry-based learning, series of reports collected and published by the Wellcome Trust.

Wenger, E. (1998) *Communities of Practice: learning, meaning and identity*, Cambridge, Cambridge University Press.

Williams, D. and Wavell, C. (2006a) *Information Literacy in the Classroom: secondary school teachers' conceptions,* Research Report 15, Aberdeen, Department of Information Management, Aberdeen Business School, The Robert Gordon University.

Williams, D. and Wavell, C. (2006b) *Untangling Spaghetti? The complexity of developing information literacy in secondary school students,* Scottish Executive Education Department, www.researchgate.net/publication/237673881_ UNTANGLING_SPAGHETTI_THE_COMPLEXITY_OF_ DEVELOPING_INFORMATION_LITERACY_IN_SECONDARY_

SCHOOL_STUDENTS (accessed 26 November 2015).

Williams, D., Wavell, C. and Morrison, K. (2013) *Impact of School Libraries on Learning: critical review of published evidence to inform the Scottish education community, final report to Scottish Library and Information Council*, Oct, http://scottishlibraries.org/wp-content/uploads/2015/05/SLIC_RGU_Impact_of_School_Libraries_2013.pdf (accessed 12 December 2015).

Wilson, P. (1983) *Second-hand Knowledge: an inquiry into cognitive authority*, Santa Barbara CA, Greenwood Press.

Index